Schöningh

Discover…

TOPICS FOR ADVANCED LEARNERS

edited by Engelbert Thaler

India
Tradition and Transformation

by Michaela Banzhaf and Alexandra Peschel

Sprachliche Betreuung: Alexandra Rieb/www.arlanguages.com

© 2008 Bildungshaus Schulbuchverlage
Westermann Schroedel Diesterweg Schöningh Winklers GmbH
Braunschweig, Paderborn, Darmstadt

www.schoeningh-schulbuch.de
Schöningh Verlag, Jühenplatz 1– 3, 33098 Paderborn

Druck 5 4 3 / Jahr 2014 13 12
Die letzte Zahl bezeichnet das Jahr dieses Druckes.

Umschlaggestaltung: Franz Josef Domke, Hannover
Umschlagabbildung: Tempel von Amritsar, picture alliance/dpa Themendienst
Druck und Bindung: westermann druck GmbH, Braunschweig

ISBN 978-3-14-040099-2

Inhaltsverzeichnis

Die didaktische Konzeption

Die Themenheftreihe *Discover ...* richtet sich an Schülerinnen und Schüler der Sekundarstufe II und bereitet in Anlehnung an die Einheitlichen Prüfungsanforderungen in der Abiturprüfung (EPA) und die Rahmenrichtlinien der einzelnen Bundesländer interkulturell relevante, Jugendliche interessierende Themen methodisch-didaktisch auf.

Der Einstieg in das Thema, das in mehrere Kapitel untergliedert ist, erfolgt über eine Doppelseite „Getting started" mit Bildmaterial und einigen Einstiegsaufgaben. Die Texte weisen unterschiedliche Längen auf, sind aber insgesamt nicht zu lang und berücksichtigen verschiedene Textsorten. Reichlich Bildmaterial (Fotos, Zeichnungen, Cartoons, Grafiken, Tabellen, Karten etc.) ist funktional in die Texte und Aufgabenapparate integriert.

Der Aufbau der einzelnen Texte ermöglicht einen klar strukturierten Unterricht mit drei Phasen: *pre*, *while* und *post reading*. *Pre-reading*-Aufgaben führen zum Text hin, rufen das Vorwissen ab und bauen Erwartungshaltungen auf. Der eigentliche Leseprozess wird im Sinne eines *guided reading* durch gelegentliche Lesebeobachtungsaufgaben und (sparsame) Annotationen in den Fußnoten unterstützt.

Im abschließenden Aufgabenapparat unter dem Titel „Activities" werden alle Fragen zu thematisch zusammengehörigen Blöcken mit einer kurzen inhaltlichen Überschrift in der Randspalte zusammengefasst. Diese Aufgaben lassen sich den drei maßgeblichen Bereichen zuordnen: a) Inhalt (*comprehension*), b) Struktur, Intention, Stil, Sprache (*analysis*), c) Evaluation, eigene Meinungsäußerung, sprachproduktive kreative Aufgaben (*evaluation and creation*). Kurze Info-Texte vermitteln überdies interessante Hintergrundinformationen und tragen zum Aufbau eines Basiswissens bei.

Prof. Dr. Engelbert Thaler, Herausgeber

Discover ... India – Tradition and Transformation

Aufbau des Schülerheftes

Thema des Heftes aus der Reihe *Discover ...* ist Indien als Land des Übergangs zwischen Tradition und Fortschritt. Diesem übergeordneten Thema wollen die einzelnen Kapitel und die darin angebotenen Texte Rechung tragen.

Die Autorinnen haben versucht, den Schülerinnen und Schülern mithilfe von vier Aspekten – *Growing up, Women, Boom Times, Bollywood* und *In Search of an Identity* – einen Einblick in Gestalt und Wesen der indischen Gesellschaft zu verschaffen und die Spannungen und Probleme, aber auch das Potenzial und die Chancen eines Landes im Umbruch zu vermitteln. Die Aufgabenapparate fordern die Schülerinnen und Schüler in vielerlei Hinsicht zum selbstorganisierten Arbeiten und zum Arbeiten im Team auf und entsprechen damit den Anforderungen der Bildungspläne.

Tabellarische Textübersicht

Autor, Text	Inhaltliche Schwerpunkte	Textsorte	Wortzahl ca.
Facts about India	• historischer, geographischer und gesellschaftlicher Überblick	Tabellen, expositorische Texte	630
Worksheet im Lehrerheft			
Worksheet 1, S. 12	Demographics for India and the European Union		

Growing up

Autor, Text	Inhaltliche Schwerpunkte	Textsorte	Wortzahl ca.
Deepti Priya Mehrotra: Girls Without Power	• Situation indischer Mädchen in ländlichen Gebieten in der Schule, in der Familie, bei der Arbeit • konkrete Benachteiligung von Mädchen in staatlichen Schulen	expositorischer Text	790
Autorentext: Perspectives for the Future?	• Kinderarbeit in Indien • Zusammenhang zwischen Verbraucherverhalten in den westlichen Industrieländern und Indien	Collage aus Text, Bildern und Statistiken	90
Aryn Baker: India's Affirmative Action War	• Quotensystem an indischen Universitäten • Proteste und Reaktionen betroffener Studenten	expositorischer Text	550
Worksheet im Lehrerheft			
Worksheet 2, S. 19	Dan McDougall: Indian "Slave" Children Found Making Low-cost Clothes Destined for Gap		

Women

Autor, Text	Inhaltliche Schwerpunkte	Textsorte	Wortzahl ca.
Amelia Gentleman: Brides Pay the Price for Indian Dowry Fever	• *dowry* als gesamtgesellschaftliches Phänomen in Indien • konkrete Beispiele negativer Folgen von *dowry* für betroffene Frauen und deren Familien • Reaktionen von Behörden auf *dowry*	Zeitungsartikel aus *International Herald Tribune*	967
Jill McGivering: India's Lost Girls	• Frauenmangel in bestimmten ländlichen Gebieten Indiens aufgrund gezielter Abtreibung weiblicher Föten und die Folgen für die indische Gesellschaft	Zeitungsartikel aus *BBC News*	438
Chitra B. Divakaruni: Arranged Marriage	• gezielte Abtreibung weiblicher Föten in Indien • Haltung bestimmter Inder zu dieser Praxis • konkrete Situation einer jungen Inderin • Kontrastierung von Lebensentwürfen zweier junger Inderinnen in den USA und in Indien	Ausschnitt aus einer Kurzgeschichte	1348
Jhumpa Lahiri: Interpreter of Maladies	• arrangierte Ehe • zwei junge Menschen erleben den Beginn ihrer arrangierten Ehe • Leben in einer bisher unbekannten Kultur	Ausschnitt aus einer Kurzgeschichte	1438
Pete Engardio: India's New Worldly Women	• veränderte Haltung, Ideale, Werte und Ziele junger indischer Frauen	Zeitungsartikel aus *The Business Week online*	678

Boom Times

Autor, Text	Inhaltliche Schwerpunkte	Textsorte	Wortzahl ca.
Why India's Hot ... How It's Changing	• Informationen zu Indiens boomender Wirtschaft • Informationen zur Verwestlichung der indischen Gesellschaft	Collage aus Text, Bildern und Statistiken	350
India's IT Industry: Dream Run	• Situation der indischen IT Industrie • Rolle von Politik und Universitäten	expositorischer Text	730
Ron Moreau/Sudip Mazumdar: Green Profits	• Modernisierung der indischen Landwirtschaft durch Investitionen von Seiten der indischen Industrie • Erschließung neuer Märkte in den ländlichen Gebieten Indiens • Rolle der indischen Politik bei der Modernisierung der indischen Landwirtschaft	expositorischer Text	790
Poverty and Despair	• verzweifelte finanzielle Situation vieler indischer Landwirte • Selbstmord als Ausweg aus der finanziellen Notlage	Collage aus Text und Bildern	230
Worksheets im Lehrerheft			
Worksheet 3, S. 46	Figures of Speech		
Worksheet 4, S. 52	Writing a Classical Speech		

Klausur im Lehrerheft	
Klausur, S. 53	Thomas L. Friedman: Bangalore: High-tech's New Hub

Bollywood

Autor, Text	Inhaltliche Schwerpunkte	Textsorte	Wortzahl ca.
Jonathan Torgovnik: Bollywood Dreams	• Überblick über die Geschichte des indischen Kinos • Stellenwert des Kinos in der indischen Gesellschaft • Charakteristika indischer Erfolgsfilme	Auszug aus einem Sachbuch	982
Malcolm Beith: The Great King Khan	• persönliche Ansichten Sharukh Khans zu bestimmten Fragen	Interview aus *Newsweek*	583

Worksheet im Lehrerheft	
Worksheet 5, S. 61	Hollywood vs Bollywood vs Kollywood

In Search of an Identity

Autor, Text	Inhaltliche Schwerpunkte	Textsorte	Wortzahl ca.
E. M. Forster: A Passage to India	• das erste Treffen der Engländerin Mrs Moore mit einem der Hauptcharaktere des Romans • "the secret understanding of the heart" • Verhältnis zwischen britischen Kolonialherren und indischer Bevölkerung	Auszug aus einem Roman	890
Mahatma Ghandi: Benaras University Speech	• Rolle der Muttersprache bei der gesellschaftlichen und politischen Konsolidierung einer Nation • Ghandis Stellungnahme zur Frage der Gewaltanwendung	Auszug aus einer Rede	700
Jhumpa Lahiri: My Two Lives	• Probleme und Chancen beim Aufwachsen in zwei Kulturen (Indien und USA) • Rolle der Eltern • Funktion von Literatur	persönliche Stellungnahme (*Newsweek*)	976

Worksheets und Klausur im Lehrerheft	
Worksheet 6, S. 68	Aziz's Language
Worksheet 7, S. 69	E. M. Forster: A Passage to India
Klausur, S. 79	Bali Rai: (Un)arranged Marriage

Weiterführende Hinweise

Getting started:
http://en.wikipedia.org → Hinduism → Ganges
http://indiantemples.com/Ganga/ganga.html
http://www.pilgrimage-india.com/holy-rivers/ganga-ganges-river.html

Growing up:
Tanuja Desai Hidier, *Born Confused*, London 2002
www.tdh.de/was-wir-tun/arbeitsfelder/kinderarbeit.html
http://www.unicef.org/india/children_2359.htm
http://www.gapinc.com → Media → Press Releases → Search: "child labor"

Women:
Anita Desai, *Clear Light of Day*, Random House, London 2001
Buchi Emecheta, *The Bride Price*, Allison & Busby, London 1976
Ruth Prawler Jhabvala, *Heat and Dust*, John Murray, London 1975
Kamala Markandaya, *Nectar in a Sieve*, Signet Classic, New York 2002
Anita Nair, *Ladies Coupé*, Vintage, London 2003
Arundhati Roy, *The God of Small Things*, Random House, New York 1997

Boom Times:
http://www.indiadaily.com/editorial/4974.asp
http://www.ieo.org/kav002.html
www.indianetzone.com/
www.nasscom.in

Bollywood:
Myriam Alexowitz, *Traumfabrik Bollywood*, Horlemann, Bad Honnef 2003
Tejaswini Ganti, *Bollywood. A Guidebook to Popular Hindi Cinema*, Routledge, New York 2004
Suketu Mehta, „Traumfabrik Hollywood", in: National Geographic (Collector's Edition No. 8), S. 96–104
Claus Tieber, *Passages to Bollywood. Einführung in den Hindi-Film*, LIT-Verlag, Münster 2007
www.filmfare.com
www.bollywood.com

In Search of an Identity:
Kindlers Neues Literaturlexikon, s. v. Edward Morgan Forster
http://www.bookrags.com/notes/pti
E. M. Forster, *A Passage to India*, Penguin Books, London 1989
David Lean (dir.): *A Passage to India*, 1984
http://www.mkgandhi.org
Richard Attenborough (dir.): *Gandhi*, 1982, starring Ben Kingsley as Gandhi
Feroze Abbas Khan (dir.): *Gandhi, My Father*, 2007

Da Indien sowohl als Urlaubsland als auch als aufstrebende Wirtschaftsmacht zurzeit in den Medien stark präsent ist, kann die Aufgabe aus dem Schülerbuch erweitert werden, indem die Schülerinnen und Schüler dazu aufgefordert werden, Bilder von Indien aus Zeitschriften und Zeitungen mitzubringen und in kurzen Statements auf Englisch zu erklären, was sie dazu bewogen hat, gerade diese Bilder auszuwählen. Auf diese Weise entsteht schon zu Beginn der Unterrichtseinheit ein sehr breit gefächertes und vermutlich auch sehr konträres Bild des indischen Subkontinents.

Die Antworten der Schülerinnen und Schüler auf Frage 1 werden zunächst an der Tafel gesammelt.

The atmosphere of the picture is:

- oriental
- colourful
- bright
- lively
- fairytale-like
- festive
- peaceful

Im Anschluss sollen die Schülerinnen und Schüler die an der Tafel gesammelten Begriffe in einen kurzen Text umsetzen.

Aufgabe 3 kann in Gruppenarbeit erledigt werden, wobei die einzelnen Gruppen den Auftrag bekommen, die Ergebnisse ihrer Arbeit im Rahmen einer Kurzpräsentation vorzustellen. Falls die Möglichkeit besteht, in die Bearbeitung dieser Aufgabe etwas mehr Zeit zu investieren, können die Gruppen verschiedene Teilaspekte des Themas, wie z. B. „Hinduism", „Pilgrimages to the Ganges", „Geographical facts of the Ganges", „The Ganges and its ecological problems" bearbeiten.

Solutions

1. **Consider the picture for one or two minutes and describe its atmosphere.**
   The atmosphere of the picture reminds one of a fairy tale. The picture looks as if it was a scene taken from one of the stories of the Arabian Nights. The colours are very bright, the sky is a clear blue and people's clothes are richly patterned. The steps leading down to the river and the building on the riverbank are old and decaying, but still show their old splendour which adds to the fairy-tale look of the scene. The scene seems to be lively and peaceful at the same time because, although there are a lot of people, they do not seem to be in a hurry. Each of them seems to be concentrated on the ritual bath they are taking or going to take in the river.

2. **Does this picture confirm or contradict your ideas about present-day India? Give reasons for your answer.**
   The picture confirms the idea of India as a place of meditation, religion and tradition where people live the way they lived centuries ago. India is shown as a country where time seems to stand still for the better of its citizens. People seem to live modest and

worry-free lives and to be satisfied with what they have. This is the image of India Europeans are familiar with from fairy tales, from adventure books, from old Hollywood and new Bollywood movies and from the brochures and commercials of travel agencies.

This image contradicts the idea of modern India in two ways. It does not show the problems of rural, present-day India, like appalling poverty, oppression of women or social inequality, nor does it show the chances of urban present-day India, as a rising economic superpower, mainly in the IT sector.

In short, it shows us what we, Europeans, expect and want to see, but it is not a faithful portrait of many-faceted modern-day India.

3. **The people in the picture are taking a ritual bath in the river Ganges. Find out more about the importance of this river in Hinduism and other religions in India.**
Individual answers

Facts About India

Unterrichtsempfehlungen

Zur Bearbeitung von Aufgabe 1 bieten neben den entsprechenden Seiten von Wikipedia folgende Internetadressen eine Fülle von Informationen:
- History: http://www.indianchild.com/history_of_india.htm
- Geography: http://www.geographia.com/india/
- Society: http://www.iloveindia.com
- Government: http://goidirectory.nic.in
- The Caste System: http://www.indianchild.com/caste_system_in_india.htm
- Genereller Überblick: http://geography.about.com/library/maps/blindia.htm.

Die Gruppenarbeit sollte arbeitsteilig angelegt werden, d.h. jede Gruppe wählt ein Thema aus, das bearbeitet wird. Die Ergebnisse der Gruppenarbeit werden im Rahmen einer Kurzpräsentation vorgestellt. Besteht die Möglichkeit, Poster im Klassenzimmer aufzuhängen, so können die wesentlichen Aspekte der jeweiligen Themen auf Postern festgehalten werden, auf die man im Laufe der Unterrichtseinheit immer wieder rekurrieren kann.

Das Zahlenmaterial für Aufgabe 2 kann in häuslicher Vorbereitung erarbeitet und im Unterricht, beispielsweise in Partnerarbeit, in die als Arbeitsblatt vorliegende Tabelle (Worksheet 1) eingetragen werden.
Im Anschluss an die Partnerarbeit erhalten die Schülerinnen und Schüler den Auftrag, die gesammelten Daten im Hinblick auf die wirtschaftliche Zukunft beider Subkontinente zu untersuchen. Dabei spielt vor allem die Altersstruktur eine Rolle. In der Diskussion ist zu betonen, dass die Prozentzahl der 15 – 64-Jährigen, also derer, die sich potenziell im Arbeitsprozess befinden, fast gleich hoch ist, die Prozentzahl der unter 15-Jährigen in Indien jedoch fast doppelt so hoch ist wie in Europa, d.h., dass in Indien ein erheblich größeres Potenzial an Arbeitskräften vorhanden ist und diese Tatsache die wirtschaftliche Entwicklung des Landes positiv beeinflussen wird. Unterstützt wird diese prognostizierte positive wirtschaftliche Entwicklung des Landes durch die flächendeckende Verbreitung des Englischen als Verkehrssprache, während in Europa nur rund die Hälfte der Bevölkerung Englisch als Zweitsprache spricht.
Am Ende der Diskussion sollen die Schülerinnen und Schüler einen resümierenden Schlusssatz formulieren und in die Kopiervorlage eintragen. Diese Schlusssätze können im Plenum vorgetragen und kurz kommentiert werden.

Solutions

1. **Choose one of the given topics. Work in small groups to get more information and prepare a presentation.**   Activities p. 8
   Individual answers

2. **Examine the above section on Indian society and find comparable material for the European Union. Compare the data and use it for a discussion of the economic future of both subcontinents. The following Internet addresses might help you:**
   http://europa.eu/index_en.htm
   http://en.wikipedia.org/wiki/Demographics_of_the_European_Union
   vgl. Unterrichtsempfehlungen

Worksheet 1

Demographics for India and the European Union

Aspects	India	Europe
Population	1.1 billion	
Age structure:		
0–14 years	31.2%	
15–64 years	63.9%	
65 years and over	4.9%	
Religion:		
Hindu	81.3%	
Muslim	12%	
Christian	2.3%	
Sikh	1.9%	
other	2.5%	
Languages:		
English	Most important language for national, political and commercial communication	
other	– Hindi: national and main language for 30% of the population – 14 other official languages	

→ Prognosis for the economic future of India and the European Union:

_____

_____

_____

Worksheet 1 Solution

Aspects	India	Europe
Population	1.1 billion	494.8 million
Age structure:		
0–14 years	31.2%	16.03%
15–64 years	63.9%	67.17%
65 years and over	4.9%	16.81%
Religion:		
Hindu	81.3%	
Muslim	12%	8%
Christian	2.3%	75% (Roman Catholic, Protestant, Orthodox)
Sikh	1.9%	
other	2.5%	less than 1% no confession: 17%
Languages:		
English	Most important language for national, political and commercial communication	Spoken by around 51% of the population (38% non-native speakers)
other	– Hindi: national and main language for 30% of the population – 14 other official languages	23 official languages German: most spoken first language (more than 18% of the population)

Girls Without Power

Deepti Priya Mehrotra

Author and text Deepty Priya Mehrotra earned a doctorate in political science from Delhi University in 1991. She works as a free journalist, author and teacher and is active in the Indian women's rights movement. Mehrotra's text is about school education for girls in India and the difficulties girls have to overcome at home and at school in order to obtain basic education. Many girls have to work to support their families besides going to school which means they have to work before and after school, and so most of them only go to school as long as it is absolutely necessary. Another difficulty is posed by the situation at schools, where girls are treated as second class pupils while boys are preferred and supported by teachers to the detriment of girls.

Unterrichtsempfehlungen

Zur Einstimmung der Schülerinnen und Schüler auf die in diesem Kapitel behandelte Thematik kann in der Klasse eine kleine Umfrage zum Thema „Frauen in Schule und Beruf" gemacht und das Ergebnis anschließend diskutiert werden. Folgende Impulsfragen können hierzu eingesetzt werden:

- (for the girls in class) Have you ever considered not going to grammar school or not having a job because you are a girl?
- How many of your mothers trained for a job?
- How many of your mothers work?
- How many of your grandmothers trained for a job?
- How many are still working or worked until their retirement?

Um die Vertraulichkeit der Informationen sicherzustellen, sollte diese Umfrage geheim gemacht werden, d.h. die Schülerinnen und Schüler schreiben ihre Antworten informell auf Zettel. Die Auswertung kann per Tafelanschrieb erfolgen.

In der anschließenden Diskussion wird vermutlich deutlich werden, dass die Zahl der arbeitenden Mütter größer ist als die der arbeitenden Großmütter, d.h. dass sich in Deutschland im Laufe der letzten 50–60 Jahre die Position der Frau in der Gesellschaft verändert hat. Ausgehend von dieser Feststellung kann zur zentralen Frage des ersten Textes übergeleitet werden: „What does education have to do with power?"

Nach dieser Diskussion folgt die Bearbeitung des ersten Textes dieses Kapitels.

Solutions

Before you read p. 9 **Concentrate on the young women in the foreground of these two pictures. Speculate on their education, their family situation and their future.**

The woman working in the fields probably only has a basic education, if any at all. She comes from a poor family with many children and probably has a family of her own. Her future life will probably be very much the same; she will continue living in a village and working on the fields to sustain her family.

The other woman is probably an IT engineer. She comes from a wealthy and not too traditional family because her family had the money and was open-minded enough to send her to school and university. She probably comes from a small, western-style family and will continue working after her own marriage. She works for one of India's IT companies and therefore belongs to the still small sector of Indian society which lives comfortable, stable and secure lives.

1. **What is the day of a girl in rural India like?**

   Activities p. 11

   Like Naina, many girls in rural India have to take jobs to support their families, which is very difficult because they have to go to school as well. They sometimes even work before school and then again after school has finished. This also means that they cannot afford to go to school for more than four or five years which severely limits their chances to be able to train for jobs, and later to obtain well-paid work.

2. **How is the government trying to improve the situation?**

   The government is trying to improve the situation of girls by setting up schools in smaller places so that girls can reach them more easily. If families cannot afford to send their daughters to school at all girls can even get scholarships and meals at schools. There are also plans for boarding schools which specialize in training girls.

3. **Describe the situation of girls at school as it is shown in the text.**

   Schools often do not welcome girls. They treat girls as second class pupils even if they are co-educational. Girls are discriminated against by not being allowed to use playgrounds or, even worse, are not given access to facilities like science labs. Teachers are only concerned with boys and neglect girls. When girls are late because they have to work before going to school, or because they have to walk long distances, they are told off.

   There are not enough female teachers who can relate to girls' problems and give them the feeling of being wanted and understood. Male teachers, on the other hand, have no notion of women's rights and the traditional ideas of a woman's role in society are even promoted in textbooks.

4. **Explain the function of the examples of girls' daily lives in the text.**

   The examples in this text are used to illustrate and underline its argument by showing exactly how difficult girls' lives are. The examples are more convincing because they are taken from real life and use names and dates of real people.

5. **Imagine you are the mother mentioned in the last paragraph of the text. Write a letter of protest to the local government. You can use the information you gathered when answering question no. 3.**

   Sita Kapoor
   Sangam Vihar
   Delhi

   Dear Sir or Madam,

   I'm writing this letter to complain about the situation of girls at Indian schools in general, and my own daughter's school in Sangam Vihar, Delhi, in particular.
   My husband and I are aware of the importance of a good education for girls in present-day India and we want our daughter to have a better life. We both work very hard to make it possible for her to go to school without having to go to work in her free time.
   However, it is all in vain because our daughter – together with all the other girls in her form – is treated like a second class pupil if she is taken seriously at all. Teachers do not support girls in their efforts to improve their education. On the contrary, they even make it more difficult for them to learn by barring them from using science labs or computers. Some teachers even refuse to talk to girls in class at all.

The textbooks my daughter uses are highly inappropriate, too, because they only show the traditional roles of men and women. Men have an education and a job; women stay at home and take care of the family. Do you think this image is still valid in the India of the 21st century, when there are so many companies desperately looking for well-educated workers – both male and female?

Another important issue is the lack of female teachers at Indian schools, because only they can relate to girls' problems and set them an encouraging example of what educated women can do with their lives.

I therefore demand modern bias-free appropriate education for boys and girls at Indian schools to pave the way into the 21st century for the whole of Indian society.

Yours faithfully,

Sita Kapoor

Perspectives for the Future?

Author and text This paragraph mainly uses pictures to convey its message, i.e. to criticise the situation of children working in Indian sweatshops to produce fake designer goods for the Western market. Students are called on to reflect on their own consumer habits and find a connection between these habits and the problem of child labour in the Third World.

The two additional texts give concrete examples of the involvement of Western clothing manufacturers in the issue of child labour in India.

Unterrichtsempfehlungen

Aufgabe 1 soll die Schülerinnen und Schüler auf die Problematik von Kinderarbeit und die Wechselwirkung zwischen westlichem Verbraucherverhalten und Produktionsbedingungen in den Ländern der 3. Welt aufmerksam machen.

Nach der vorbereitenden Recherche nach Produkten aus der 3. Welt im eigenen Zimmer soll im Unterrichtsgespräch geklärt werden, weshalb Produkte aus der 3. Welt für westliche Käufer so attraktiv sind und inwiefern unser Kaufverhalten, z.B. die Nachfrage nach billigen, gefälschten Markenprodukten, die Situation der Arbeitnehmer in den Ländern der 3. Welt beeinflusst.

Folgende Impulsfragen können für diese Diskussion eingesetzt werden:

- What products do you have that were produced in the Third World?
- Why is it so important to wear or own fake designer goods?
- Are you interested in *where* the goods you buy were produced?
- Would you refrain from buying something if you knew it was produced by children?
- In how far do or can we influence markets and working conditions in the Third World?
- Are there any alternatives to your present behaviour as a consumer?

Die Ergebnisse der Diskussion von Aufgabe 1 und 2 können in folgendes Tafelbild münden.

Western consumer habits		Third World working conditions
– cheap products of high quality	**negative**	– long working hours
– cheap fakes of products of high quality	**→**	– poor working conditions
	influence	– cheap workers (often children)
$\updownarrow$		$\updownarrow$
– decent price-value relationship	**positive**	– appropriate working hours
	→	– improved working conditions
	influence	– fair wages: workers can sustain their families, child labour becomes unnecessary

Die unter Aufgabe 3 angegebenen Internetseiten bieten eine Fülle von Informationen zum Thema „Kinderarbeit". Es ist daher sinnvoll, die genannten Details in Kleingruppen aufbereiten und präsentieren zu lassen.

Folgende Gruppenthemen sind denkbar:

- child protection
- improving education
- child labour
- measures which customers can take to stop child labour
- measures which governments can take to stop child labour
- projects for working children

In die Bearbeitung von Aufgabe 4 können die Ergebnisse der Beschäftigung mit den Texten des gesamten Kapitels einmünden.

Eine Organisation als Klassenprojekt ist hier sinnvoll, in dem sich verschiedene Gruppen mit den verschiedenen Publikationsformen (Fernsehspot, Annonce, Poster) beschäftigen. Eine Abstimmung untereinander ist dann sinnvoll, wenn die Einzelergebnisse zu einer „Medienkampagne" zusammengefasst werden sollen, die dann in der Schule ausgestellt werden kann. Eine fächerübergreifende Zusammenarbeit mit den Fächern der Gesellschaftswissenschaften (Religion, Ethik, Gemeinschaftskunde) ist denkbar.

Zur Vertiefung des Themas „Kinderarbeit in Indien" kann der Zusatztext über das Modelabel Gap (Worksheet 2) eingesetzt werden.

Solutions

1. **Inspect your wardrobe and your room: which of the things you own might have been produced in third world countries and therefore possibly by children?**
   Individual answers

   Activities p. 12

2. **Do you prefer special brands – and if so, why? Discuss your shopping habits in small groups and explain how consumer habits in the Western world influence the production and working conditions in developing countries.**
   Individual answers

3. **Search the Internet for international organizations which are concerned with education. The following pages might help you:**
   www.tdh.de/was-wir-tun/arbeitsfelder/kinderarbeit.html
   http://www.unicef.org/india/children_2359.htm
   Individual answers

4. **Work in groups to develop a campaign (TV spots, adverts, posters) to make people in industrial countries aware of the problem of child labour and poor education. You may use your findings from the previous tasks, along with the information and pictures in this chapter, and other sources.**
Creative task

Worksheet 2

Indian "Slave" Children Found Making Low-cost Clothes Destined for Gap

Dan McDougall

Child workers, some as young as 10, have been found working in a textile factory in conditions close to slavery to produce clothes that appear destined for Gap Kids, one of the most successful arms[1] of the high street giant.

Speaking to *The Observer*, the children described long hours of unwaged[2] work as well
5 as threats and beatings.

Gap said it was unaware[3] that clothing intended for the Christmas market had been improperly subcontracted[4] to a sweatshop[5] using child labour. It announced it had withdrawn the garments[6] involved while it investigated breaches of the ethical code imposed by it three years ago.

10 The discovery of the children working in filthy[7] conditions in the Shapur Jat area of Delhi has renewed concerns about the outsourcing by large retail chains of their garment production to India, recognised by the United Nations as the world's capital for child labour. According to one estimate, more than 20 per cent of India's economy is dependent on children, the equivalent of 55 million youngsters under 14.

15 The Observer discovered the children in a filthy sweatshop working on piles[8] of beaded[9] children's blouses marked with serial numbers that Gap admitted corresponded with its own inventory[10]. The company has pledged[11] to convene[12] a meeting of its Indian suppliers as well as withdrawing tens of thousands of embroidered[13] girls' blouses from the market, before they reach the stores. The hand-stitched[14] tops, which
20 would have been sold for about £20, were destined for shelves in America and Europe in the next seven days in time to be sold to Christmas shoppers. [...]

Despite its charitable activities, Gap has been criticised for outsourcing large contracts to the developing world. In 2004, when it launched its social audit[15], it admitted that forced labour, child labour, wages below the minimum wage, physical punish-
25 ment and coercion[16] were among abuses it had found at some factories producing garments for it. It added that it had terminated[17] contracts with 136 suppliers as a consequence.

In the past year Gap has severed[18] contracts with a further 23 suppliers for workplace abuses. Gap said in a statement from its headquarters in San Francisco: "We firmly
30 believe that under no circumstances is it acceptable for children to produce or work on garments. These allegations[19] are deeply upsetting[20] and we take this situation very seriously. All of our suppliers and their subcontractors are required to guarantee that they will not use child labour to produce garments. In this situation, it's clear one of our vendors[21] violated this agreement and a full investigation is under way."
35 [...]

Dan McDougall, *The Observer*, October 28, 2007,
Copyright Guardian News & Media Ltd. 2007.

---

[1]**arm** branch   [2]**unwaged** unpaid   [3]**unaware** not aware, not knowing   [4]**to subcontract sth.** to give a contract to sb. else to do the work   [5]**sweatshop** factory where workers are employed, often illegally, and have to work long hours in bad working conditions for little money   [6]**garment** piece of clothing   [7]**filthy** very dirty   [8]**pile** number of things lying on top of each other   [9]**beaded** decorated with beads (*Zierperlen*)   [10]**inventory** list of goods   [11]**to pledge** to promise solemnly   [12]**to convene a meeting** to call a meeting   [13]**to embroider** to decorate with special stitches in different material, *besticken*   [14]**hand-stitched** here: hand-made   [15]**audit** examination of the state of sth.   [16]**coercion** the act of making sb. do sth. by using threats or force   [17]**to terminate** to end   [18]**to sever** to end a relationship or action   [19]**allegation** statement made without proof   [20]**upsetting** disturbing, worrying   [21]**vendor** sb. who sells sth.

Worksheet 2

Activities

1. Describe the working conditions in sweatshops where children produce clothes for companies like Gap Kids.

2. Explain how Gap products could be produced in sweatshops despite the company's ethical code.

3. Analyze the steps taken by Gap to counter child labour.

4. Use this text to devise a code of ethics for companies like Gap.

Worksheet 2 Solution

1. **Describe the working conditions in sweatshops where children produce clothes for companies like Gap Kids.**

   The children working for Gap Kids were found in a dirty sweatshop in Shapur Jat, a part of Delhi. When asked by reporters, they said they had to work long hours without payment and were threatened and even beaten. Some of the children were only ten years old.

2. **Explain how Gap products could be produced in sweatshops despite the company's ethical code.**

   Gap says the children's clothes discovered in a Delhi sweatshop by reporters of the British newspaper – *The Guardian* – were subcontracted to this sweatshop without Gap's knowledge.

   This means, that Gap placed an order for the production of children's tops with a clothing factory, which in turn passed parts of the production or the whole production onto a sweatshop.

3. **Analyze the steps taken by Gap to counter child labour.**

   Gap took several steps to limit the damage done to its reputation by the discovery of Gap products in an Indian sweatshop which employed children. The company withdrew the clothes in question from the market and called a meeting of all its Indian suppliers to discuss the issue. Gap also tries to make sure that children do not work for the company by making its suppliers and subcontractors guarantee that they will not employ children in their factories.

4. **Use this text to devise a code of ethics for companies like Gap.**

   Für die Bearbeitung dieser Aufgabe bietet es sich an, die Klasse in Gruppen zu unterteilen, die ihre Ergebnisse im Anschluss an die Gruppenarbeitsphase im Plenum diskutieren.

   Code of Ethics
   1. Orders must not be subcontracted to other companies without the client's knowledge
   2. Producers must not employ children under the age of 15.
   3. Producers must pay their employees appropriate wages and must guarantee safe and healthy working conditions.
   4. Goods produced in factories which do not live up to the standards stated above are not to be sold in our shops.
   5. Contracts with factories which do not accept the standards set above will be severed immediately.

India's Affirmative Action War

Aryn Baker

Author and text

Aryn Baker is associate editor of the Asian edition of *Time Magazine* based in Hong Kong. She has earned an MA in journalism from the University of California.

Baker's text is about the quota system for lower caste students at Indian Universities which is increasingly criticized by both upper and lower caste students. While students from the upper castes fear that they are disadvantaged because certain quotas of places at universities are given to lower caste students and so their own chances of earning a place at university are diminished, lower caste students want to be accepted into university because of their talents and achievements and not because of belonging to a certain caste.

Background information

The Indian constitution prohibits any discrimination based on religion, caste, race, sex, and place of birth. But the Indian constitution also contains a sort of "positive discrimination", to ensure reservation "for the advancement of any socially and educationally backward classes of citizens or for the Scheduled Castes and Tribes to ensure their political representation for 10 years." This policy has been continued up to the present. So there is a quota system for members of lower castes in the Parliament of India, state legislative assemblies, central and state civil services, public sector units, central and state government departments, and in all public and private educational institutions.

Unterrichtsempfehlungen

In einem einleitenden Unterrichtsgespräch können die Faktoren für eine erfolgreiche Karriere erarbeitet und an der Tafel festgehalten werden.

Preconditions for a successful career

– good education at school
– foreign language competence, mainly in English
– mobility
– ambition
– support from one's family

Die individuellen Interpretationen des Slogans von Aufgabe 4 sollen Grundlage der Diskussion sein. Folgende Impulsfragen können weiterhin hilfreich sein:
– In how far does the political system of a democracy support the idea of merit as it is shown in the text?
– Are there any fields in our society where class and background are still important?
– Have you ever experienced such a situation?
– What is the basis for a career in our society? – Think of your answers to the lead-in question.

Die Diskussion kann in folgendes Tafelbild münden:

"Merit is my caste"

merit: hard work, ambition
caste: opportunities in life, success

↓

merit:		**caste:**
– hard work	=	– opportunities in life
– ambition		– success

Schülerinnen und Schüler am Gymnasium müssen für das Problem der Ungleichheit der Bildungschancen auch in unserer Gesellschaft (Aufgabe 5) oft erst sensibilisiert werden, da es für sie selbstverständlich ist, eine weiterführende Schule zu besuchen und einen Bildungsabschluss zu erwerben, der sie für alle weiteren Bildungseinrichtungen qualifiziert. Hilfreich für die Diskussion ist es sicherlich, wenn einige Denkanstöße gegeben werden:

Think about the factors which determine success at school and in job training:
– a sound financial background
– being integrated in German society
– speaking German

Die anschließende Diskussion findet in Kleingruppen statt, wobei jede Gruppe den Auftrag erhält, das Ergebnis ihrer Diskussion graphisch darzustellen.

Aufgabe 6 kann als das Kapitel abschließende und zusammenfassende Hausaufgabe erteilt werden.

Solutions

1. Why are so many students of elite universities protesting against quotas for lower caste students?

Activities p. 14

The quota system was introduced to overcome the inequality of Indian society where, even today, people coming from lower castes suffer from disadvantages compared to members of higher castes. However, many students feel this system is highly unjust because they say that the only thing that qualifies a person to go to university is what they, themselves, are able to achieve. Preferring students from lower castes is as discriminating as preferring students from higher castes.

2. What are the implications of "caste" in Indian society?

The caste you were born into is still of great importance in Indian society. It is obvious in your name, your family background and your own personal identity. On the surface of urban Indian society it does not play a role any more, but the caste your marriage partner belongs to is still important. The situation is completely different in more rural areas where the caste you belong to determines a great part of your future life.

3. How do lower caste students react to the quota system?

Surprisingly enough, even lower caste students who benefit from the quota regulation, reject it because they do not want to be accepted into universities simply because of their belonging to a lower caste. They want to prove their aptitude by the quality of their work.

4. "Merit is my caste." Write down your interpretation of this motto in a few sentences, then hold a discussion in class about whether this motto is valid in our society.

In India, the caste you were born into is a decisive factor in shaping your future life. It determines which education you will have, which jobs you will get and whom you will be able to marry or associate with. In short, it determines the chances and opportunities in your life and whether or not you will be successful.

"Merit is my caste" argues that it is not social background which determines a person's life but the person's own merit or achievements. So what is really important is what one is capable of and ready to do.

5. Which groups in German society are disadvantaged when it comes to education? Devise a plan to improve the situation.

Abolishing disadvantages in the German educational system

reasons	remedies	results
– poverty	– creating new jobs – providing financial support, e. g. scholarships, loans for students, etc.	– sound financial basis for sending children to school and university
– no integration in German society and its value systems	– offering free, possibly compulsory, integration courses – breaking down prejudices e. g. by media campaigns	– having a cultural education which will foster a sense of security in German society
– poor knowledge of the German language	– offering language classes for parents and children	– essential basis for education and learning in the German education system

6. Imagine you were a civil servant in the education authorities. Use the information from the texts in this chapter so far and write an official report on the educational reality of the "lower castes and classes" in India today.

The educational reality of lower castes and classes in India

The problems in the education system in India today come down to two important issues: gender and caste – which are often interrelated and especially obvious in rural India. Let me begin with the former issue first. While boys enjoy at least some basic education in local schools, the situation of girls is desperate. First, there are personal reasons which make it very difficult for girls to pursue a career at school. Many girls have to contribute to their families' living and so have to go to work besides going to school. They sometimes even work before and after school which means they often arrive late and are too exhausted to follow classes. Even if their parents see the necessity of learning for their daughters and are willing to send them to school, their efforts often remain fruitless because of the situation at schools. There are not enough female teachers who can relate to girls' problems. Male teachers often neglect their female pupils and concentrate solely on the boys in the classroom. Girls get the impression they are not wanted and not taken seriously. This impression is intensified by the books which are used in classes, in which girls practically never appear. Girls are often banned from rooms with special equipment like science or computer rooms and are thus put at a great disadvantage. Even worse, girls are bullied and verbally abused, not only by their male classmates, but even by their male teachers.

The second important issue is caste. It is vital that members of all castes should have the possibility to attend school and that their schooling should not be restricted to primary school but should embrace the complete educational system in the country. This way there would not be troubles at universities like the ones we have just witnessed. If everybody had the same chance to go to school, we would not need a quota system for members of the lower castes in India, and there would be no feeling of injustice in all the parties involved.

So to sum up it is of great importance that every citizen of the country, no matter what gender and what caste they belong to, should have the right to attend school and be appropriately educated. Only if we can achieve this, will we lead India into a socially stable and economically prosperous future.

Brides Pay the Price for Indian Dowry Fever

Amelia Gentleman

Amelia Gentleman is a correspondent for the *Observer* and for the *International Herald Tribune*. In February 2005 she moved to Delhi to start work as a New Delhi correspondent. She has won three awards for her coverage of India. She won first prize for feature writing in the 2007 Human Rights Press Awards organized by Amnesty International Hong Kong. The article taken from the *International Herald Tribune* (23.10.2006) informs the reader about dowry practices currently existent in India. Although the giving and taking of dowry is forbidden by law, it is widely practised, with people becoming ever more aggressive and greedy; dowry is perceived as an easy means to fulfil personal materialistic needs. The bride's family is forced to satisfy the ever growing and exaggerated claims of the groom and his family, violence being an omnipresent means to make demands more urgent. As a last resort very many young women consider suicide.

Author and text

Obwohl per Gesetz verboten, ist es in Indien auch heutzutage noch üblich, dass die Familie der Braut eine beträchtliche Mitgift, *dowry*, an den Bräutigam und dessen Familie entrichtet. Viele Familien werden dadurch in größte finanzielle Schwierigkeiten gestürzt. Um ihre Herkunftsfamilien vor weiteren maßlosen Forderungen zu bewahren, sehen viele der jungen Frauen keinen anderen Ausweg als Selbstmord.

Background information

Unterrichtsempfehlungen

Der Einstieg in den Text kann über einen Bildimpuls erfolgen. Damit sichergestellt werden kann, dass sich die Schülerinnen und Schüler vorab nicht vom Text beeinflussen lassen, erscheint es sinnvoll, die Abbildung auf S. 15 im Schülerbuch auf eine Folie zu kopieren und der Klasse auf dem OHP zu zeigen. Im Unterrichtsgespräch kann die Einstiegsaufgabe („Before you read") gelöst werden.
Bevor zum Text übergeleitet wird empfiehlt es sich, den Begriff „dowry" zu klären. Hierzu ist es denkbar, den gesamten Ausdruck „Indian Dowry Fever" auf eine Folie zu schreiben und zunächst nur das Wort „fever" aufzudecken, das die Schülerinnen und Schüler erklären. Danach wird der Begriff „dowry" aufgedeckt, der von der Lehrkraft erläutert werden muss.
Zum Schluss wird der gesamte Ausdruck „Indian Dowry Fever" aufgedeckt. Auf der Grundlage dessen, was bisher erklärt wurde, spekuliert die Klasse über den Inhalt des gesamten Ausdrucks. Die Lehrkraft hält die Schülerhypothesen an der Tafel fest.
Danach lesen die Schülerinnen und Schüler den Text still. Nach der Lektüre vergleichen sie den tatsächlichen Inhalt des Textes mit ihren Mutmaßungen.

Mögliches Tafelbild:

Fever: is an illness; your body temperature rises; when it has reached a certain degree, you begin to hallucinate and are not able to think clearly any more; when the temperature exceeds a certain limit, you die
Dowry: is the property and money a woman and her family give to her husband and his family when they get married
Indian Dowry Fever: Indian people pay a lot of dowry when getting married.

Möglicherweise wollen die Schülerinnen und Schüler bereits an dieser Stelle ihre Meinung zum indischen dowry-System und ihre Betroffenheit darüber äußern. Das kann in einem spontanen Unterrichtsgespräch erfolgen.

Da der Text relativ lang ist, werden die Aufgaben 1, 2 und 4 praktischerweise in differenzierter Gruppenarbeit beantwortet. Um die Ergebnisse später für die ganze Klasse verfügbar zu machen, wird jeder Gruppe zur Fixierung ihrer Ergebnisse – es genügen Stichworte – eine Folie ausgehändigt, anhand derer im Plenum berichtet wird. Die Folien können später für alle kopiert werden.

Bei Aufgabe 3 handelt es sich um eine Rechercheaufgabe, die optimalerweise als Hausaufgabe bearbeitet wird. Die Schülerinnen und Schüler bereiten zur Präsentation z. B. Plakate vor, die sich nach der Vorstellung an die Pinwand des Klassenzimmers heften lassen. Zur Bearbeitung von Aufgabe 5 bietet sich eine Pyramidendiskussion an. Zunächst machen sich die Schülerinnen und Schüler einzeln Gedanken über das Statement „Having a daughter in India is a curse" und halten diese stichwortartig fest. Danach tauschen sie sich mit ihrem Nachbarn aus und halten fest, worauf sie sich in der Zweiergruppe verständigen. Anschließend erfolgen Meinungsaustausch und kurzes Notizenmachen in der Vierergruppe. Nach angemessener Diskussionszeit trägt ein Mitglied der Gruppe die Ergebnisse vor. Danach kann eine weitere Diskussion im Plenum erfolgen. Aufgabe 6 bearbeiten die Schülerinnen und Schüler schriftlich in Einzelarbeit, optimalerweise zu Hause. Damit sich bei der Präsentation im Unterricht möglichst viele Schülerinnen und Schüler beteiligen können, werden sie aufgefordert, sich ihren Text zwei Minuten lang anzusehen. Danach nennt jeder Schüler gemäß des Blitzlichtverfahrens das Argument, das ihm am schlagendsten erscheint. Ist das Argument bereits von jemand anderem genannt worden, wird auf die/den Betreffende(n) verwiesen und zusätzlich ein weiteres hinzugefügt.

Zur Bearbeitung von Aufgabe 7 bekommen die Schülerinnen und Schüler wenige Minuten Zeit, um sich Stichworte zu notieren. Danach werden sie von der Lehrkraft in ein Kugellager zum gegenseitigen Meinungsaustausch gerufen. Um die Ideen der gesamten Gruppe zusammenzuführen, bekommen die Schülerinnen und Schüler etwa drei bis fünf Kärtchen, die sie beschriften und danach an der Tafel clustern. Danach machen sie sich an die schriftliche Ausformulierung der Aufgabe, die auch als Hausaufgabe erfolgen kann.

Folgende Beschriftungen/Cluster an der Tafel sind denkbar:

- Dowry is outdated and old-fashioned.
- Parents with daughters are discriminated against, so dowry is unjust.
- Dowry places women in a passive role; therefore it should be abolished.
- As most women work nowadays, there is no need to make their families contribute to their living.
- Today men and women have equal duties and rights – where does dowry come into this?

Solutions

Before you read p. 15 **Describe the photo. How do you feel about this scene? Speculate on how the owner came into possession of the motorbike and the TV.**

The photo shows a bare room. Apart from two relatively large devices serving as sideboards or mere decoration located in a corner of the room, an umbrella fixed to a hook on the wall and some connecting wires, we can see a TV set on one of the large devices. Obviously the motorbike and the TV set don't fit the bare room; these two items of relatively sophisticated consumer goods are in plain contrast with the very simple room. Moreover, it is surprising to find a motorbike indoors. It seems as if two different ways of life are clashing together. Maybe the owner of the motorbike and the TV set bought these objects after saving money for a very long time. Maybe he won them in a lottery or in a competition, maybe he stole them, maybe he inherited them.

1. **Describe the situation Kamlesh and her family are in.**
   Activities p. 17
   Kamlesh is an 18-year-old bride whose father, Misrilal, has offered a certain sum of money and various commodities as dowry gifts to the groom. Although Misrilal had been saving money for Kamlesh's wedding and dowry for over six years – he offered 51,000 rupees, a new TV set, a sofa and other pieces of furniture, kitchen equipment and jewellery to the groom – his gifts were not enough. The husband's family had been making demands for more dowry since the beginning of the marriage. Finally Kamlesh's husband turned to using violence against her in order to make his demands more explicit. Kamlesh is in danger of suffering permanent brain damage after her husband's violent attack against her.

2. **Explain how dowry is perceived by families and authorities in Indian society.**
   For Indians, dowry plays an important part in wedding arrangements. As dowry is officially forbidden by the authorities, Indian families refer to it as a "wedding gift". Authorities have officially prohibited giving and accepting dowry: violations of this rule can entail five years of jail, but in daily life, this punishment is never applied. So, dowry remains current practice in Indian society.

3. **Outline the work done by the Delhi Commission for Women according to the text. Next, find out about more projects carried out by it. The following Internet address might be of some help:**
   http://delhi.gov.in/wps/wcm/connect/Lib_DCW/dcw/home
   The Delhi Commission for Women is an organization paid for by the Indian government. It offers women protection from violent husbands and helps them take steps against them.

4. **Analyze how dowry demands initially developed in the past.**
   Over the last few years dowry demands have become more and more extravagant, and the means of extracting these dowry demands have become more and more violent. Nowadays Indian society is faced by violent dowry harassment: every 77 minutes an Indian woman is killed because of excessive dowry demands according to the National Crime Record Bureau. The reason for the exaggerated and growingly violent dowry demands is, according to Kiran Walia, a chairwoman of the Delhi Commission for women, a sharp rise in materialism in India. Consumerism, modelled after the Western world, is taking the lead in India.

5. **Discuss Misrilal's statement that having a daughter in India is a curse.**
   Misrilal is the father of Kamlesh, an 18-year-old daughter who was married three years ago. As the father of the bride, Misrilal had to pay for the wedding ceremony and for the dowry. The costs for the ceremony amounted to 250,000 rupees, 60,000 of which he had to borrow from his boss. Even now, years after the wedding, he is faced with important dowry demands from his son-in-law's family. Aware of the dowry Kamlesh would require, Misrilal had started saving money for his daughter when she was only a very small child. Throughout his life he had been making sacrifices for his daughter's wedding, and even after she was married he has had to go on paying and probably will have to go on giving money to his daughter's in-laws. The financial sacrifices seem endless and that is why Misrilal states "having a daughter in India is a curse".

6. **Comment on Ashram's utterance "Dowry should be abolished. Why should you give the husband's family money when you are already giving them a girl?"**

In my opinion Ashram is absolutely right. The young woman comes to live with her new husband and his family; she's supposed to do work in her new family and to obey her husband and her in-laws. Paying money to the husband's family humiliates the woman even more; she is considered an unworthy being no one bothers to take care of if they are not given money to make up for the inconvenience of accepting a young woman in their household. We must not forget that we are dealing with arranged marriages.

Choosing a woman you are in love with and treating her as your equal is not at all the underlying concept. It is bad enough for the woman not to be able to choose a partner by herself, but having to pay money to her husband's family is not at all acceptable.

7. **From your "western" perspective reflect on the dowry system.**

In the past, brides in Western societies were supposed to be equipped with a dowry as well. But this practice has gradually vanished. A significant difference to the Indian dowry system, however, was that the husband and his family couldn't ask for more and more money, even years after the wedding. In modern Western civilization this concept is considered old-fashioned and out-dated and doesn't fit our understanding of the role men and women have in present-day society.

We consider men and women as partners with equal rights and duties; the woman isn't dependent on the man any longer. Women do the same jobs as men, they earn their own money and men sometimes stay at home looking after the children, doing household chores. Women do not have to wait until men propose to them and they can take the active role in proposing. So there is no longer any need for a woman to have a dowry to contribute her share to the new common household. That's why, from a modern Western perspective, the dowry system is shocking and absolutely unacceptable because it puts women at a great disadvantage.

India's Lost Girls

Jill McGivering

Author and text   Jill McGivering works for the BBC. In May 2000 she was appointed as the BBC's South Asia correspondent, based in Delhi. Prior to this she held BBC correspondent positions in Hong Kong, Macau and Taiwan. The text reports on a horrible practice still carried out in contemporary Indian society: female foeticide. As Indians prefer boys to girls, modem technology (pre-natal scans) is used to single out female foetuses and abort them. As a result Indian society is lacking young women and young men are not able to find a wife. Because of this men are willing to marry girls from poor regions.

Unterrichtsempfehlungen

Das exotisch anmutende Foto eignet sich als visueller Impuls zum Einstieg in den Text. Im Unterrichsgespräch beschreiben die Schülerinnen und Schüler das Bild und tragen ihre Ideen zusammen, bei welchem Anlass es möglicherweise aufgenommen wurde.

Die Schülerinnen und Schüler lesen den Text still und geben seinen Inhalt mündlich in einem Satz wieder.

Aufgaben 1 und 2 können schriftlich in arbeitsteiliger Gruppenarbeit beantwortet werden.

Aufgabe 3 eignet sich zur Schulung des mündlichen Ausdrucksvermögens. Die Schülerinnen und Schüler werden aufgefordert, ein einminütiges Statement über die Praxis des Brautkaufs vorzubereiten. Dabei dürfen sie stichwortartige Notizen machen und diese bei ihrem Vortrag verwenden. Nach angemessener Vorbereitungszeit tragen sie während der einminütigen Redezeit ihre Einschätzungen vor. Die vorgegebene Zeit muss exakt eingehalten werden, darf also weder über- noch unterschritten werden. Ein zu diesem Zweck vorher bestimmter Zeitwächter kontrolliert die Einhaltung der Zeitvorgabe.

In sehr leistungsstarken Gruppen kann eine gestaffelte Redezeit angesetzt werden: der erste Sprecher spricht 30 Sekunden, der zweite 40 Sekunden usw. Es wird eine Höchstzeit festgelegt. Wer wie lange zu sprechen hat, entscheidet ein von den Schülern gezogenes Kärtchen. Um die Vorträge zeitlich nicht allzu lange auszudehnen, kann die Lehrkraft entsprechende viele „stumme Kärtchen" einfügen. In häuslicher Arbeit recherchieren die Schülerinnen und Schüler zur vorgegebenen Fragestellung in Aufgabe 5. Als Hilfestellung kann ihnen folgende Internetadresse genannt werden: www.netdoktor.de

Als Hilfestellung zu Aufgabe 6 können den Schülerinnen und Schülern Surftipps gegeben werden, z.B. das Anklicken des Buttons „Info by country", dann die Eingabe „female foeticide" als Suchwort. Es sollten alle aufgeführten Seiten berücksichtigt werden.

Solutions

Describe the photo. Speculate on what occasion it might have been taken.

In the photo we can only see the bottom part of a person. The picture shows the border of a long red garment with golden embroidery and a pair of naked feet which are decorated with jewellery; the nails are varnished in red. This makes the onlooker assume that the person shown is a woman. The photo might have been taken at a wedding ceremony or a performance.

Before you read p. 18

1. Outline the current practice in Indian hospitals („Geburtskliniken") with regard to pre-natal scans.

As people in India prefer boys to girls, modern technology is used in hospitals in order to find out via pre-natal scans if the baby to be born is a boy or a girl. If it is a girl, it is very often aborted. Although this practice of using pre-natal scans in order to kill unborn girls is forbidden by law, it is common practice to warn future parents of the sex of their unborn child.

Activities p. 19

2. Describe the consequences of this practice.

As female foetuses are aborted in large numbers, the female sector of the population is shrinking drastically. There is an acute gender imbalance. In consequence, young men are not able to find a woman to marry. So they are forced to buy a woman from a poor region.

3. Assess the practice of buying brides.

Although the practice of buying a bride has become a sheer necessity for young men in large parts of India where the proportion of females has drastically fallen, it is humiliating. Women are not considered as human beings, but rather as goods. Nobody takes into account how they feel, nobody asks if they want to leave their region and the purchaser is only interested in the woman's reproductive capacities. This makes me think of a cattle market.

4. **Explain why the whole region is "on course for catastrophe".**

   Because of the massive abortion of female foetuses, the sex ratio in India is highly imbalanced. Women are missing and young men are forced to find or rather to buy their future wives in different areas. If the abortion practice goes on like this, ever more women will be missing, and it will become ever more difficult for men to find a wife and found a family. The worst consequence could be the extinction of the Indian people.

5. **Research under which circumstances abortion is legal in your country.**

   Abortion in Germany is legal if the woman is pregnant after being raped. Abortion is also legal where there are specific medical indications. Furthermore, there is the "Beratungsregelung". The following conditions must be fulfilled in order to carry out an abortion: the woman must have had consultation and has to show the document she gets from the consultation to the doctor. The earliest date for an abortion is four days after the compulsory consultation. Abortion is only allowed up to a maximum of twelve weeks after conception (vgl. www.teenager-ratgeber.de).

   Hinweis: Literarisch wird die Thematik des Schwangerschaftsabbruchs behandelt in John Irving, The Cider House Rules (1985), in deutscher Übersetzung bekannt als „Gottes Werk und Teufels Beitrag". Der Roman wurde 1999 verfilmt mit Michael Caine, Charlize Theron und Toby Maguire.

6. **Find out the exact number of girls killed in India. The address www.unicef.org might help you.**

   Various estimates set the number of girls killed by abortion in India over the last 20 years at 10 million.

Arranged Marriage

Chitra Banerjee Divakaruni

Author and text Chitra Banerjee Divakaruni (born in 1956 in Kolkata) is an Indian-American author, poet and professor of English at the University of Houston Creative Writing Program. She is also a co-founder and former president of a helpline that assists South Asian women who are dealing with various forms of abuse from others.

Divakaruni's work has been published in over 50 magazines and her writing has been included in over 30 anthologies. While many of her novels are written for adults, she has also written the first two books of a juvenile fantasy series called "The Brotherhood of the Conch" which, like many of her adult novels, take place in India (as well as other parts of Asia and the Middle East) and draw on the culture and folklore of that region. In the extract of the short story "The Ultrasound" the reader overhears two conversations: the first, on the phone between Runu, a young Indian woman living in India with her in-laws and Anju and Sunil, a young Indian married couple living in the US; the second, between Anju and her husband. Runu and Anju have been friends since they were young girls. Now, they are both pregnant. Runu – so the amniocentesis has shown – is expecting a baby girl. Her husband and in-laws want her to abort, whereas she wants to keep the baby. In her despair she has also asked her mother for advice but has been told to do what her husband's family expect her to do. As a last resort, Runu phones Anju who advises her not to accept the in-laws' order. She advises her friend to go to her own mother for help.

In the second part of the conversation, Anju and Sunil talk to each other. Anju hoped for support from Sunil, but her husband sees things from the point of view of Runu's in-laws. Anju is shocked and asks if Sunil would have wanted her to have an abortion too, if the baby she is expecting hadn't turned out to be a boy.

Der Roman „(Un-)arranged marriages" von Bali Rai (2001) beleuchtet das Thema aus der Sicht eines männlichen Protagonisten, vgl. Klausur S. 82.   **Background information**

Unterrichtsempfehlungen

Als Einstieg ist ein Anknüpfen an die persönliche Lebenswirklichkeit der Schülerinnen und Schüler denkbar. Auf einem gesonderten Blatt skizzieren sie, ohne dabei ihren Namen zu nennen, wie sie sich als Kind ihr zukünftiges Leben als Erwachsene vorstellen bzw. vorgestellt haben. Alle Blätter werden eingesammelt und neu verteilt. Der gezogene Text wird vorgelesen, der-/diejenige, der/die ihn gezogen hat, versucht den Verfasser/die Verfasserin zu erraten. Falls das nicht gelingt, hilft die ganze Klasse mit. Der/die Erratene fährt mit dem von ihm/ihr gezogenen Text fort. Danach wird zum Text übergeleitet. Seine Länge lässt eine Behandlung in mehreren Schritten sinnvoll erscheinen. Die Struktur des Textes legt eine erste Unterbrechung der Lektüre bei Zeile 36 nahe. Die Schülerinnen und Schüler bekommen den Auftrag, diesen Teil des Textes nach den wichtigsten Informationen zu scannen, an der Tafel wird anschließend zusammengetragen. Eine entsprechende Arbeitsanweisung könnte lauten:
– Scan the Text up to line 36 for the most important information.
Das entsprechende Tafelbild kann wie folgt aussehen:

– Two friends, Anju and Runu, are talking on the phone.
– Anju lives in the US; Runu doesn't.
– They talk about an abortion Runu is supposed to have because the baby she is expecting is a girl.
– Runu is desperate.

Eine weitere Zäsur kann bei Zeile 66 erfolgen. Die *scanning*-Aufgabe wird fortgeführt, die neu gewonnenen Informationen werden an der Tafel komplettiert. Gemäß der Technik des verzögerten Lesens stellen die Schülerinnen und Schüler Mutmaßungen an, welchen Rat Anju ihrer Freundin wohl gegeben haben könnte. Die Schülerinnen und Schüler werden aufgefordert, hier an bereits behandelte Texte zu denken, z. B. S. 17, Aufgabe 3.
Das fortgeführte Tafelbild könnte wie folgt aussehen:

– Runu refuses to have an abortion.
– She considers leaving her husband and in-laws.
– She doesn't know where to go to and what to do since her mother told her to accept her in-laws' decision.
– Anju is also pregnant.

Auf die Frage „What might Anju's advice be?" könnten die Schülerinnen und Schüler äußern:
– Runu should come to Anju's place.
– She should seek advice at the Delhi Social Welfare Advisory Board or a comparable institution.
– Runu should go to a friend's house.

Der letzte Teil des Textes wird unter Beibehaltung der *scanning*-Aufgabe gelesen. Die Ergänzung des Tafelanschriebs könnte lauten:

– Anju has advised her friend to go to her own mother's house.
– There is a dispute between Anju and her husband Sunil since Sunil defends Runu's in-laws.
– Anju accuses her husband of hypocrisy.

Durch die sukzessive Informationsentnahme aus dem Text bearbeiten die Schülerinnen und Schüler Aufgabe 1 automatisch.

Die Länge des Textes legt die Beantwortung der Aufgabe 2 in gruppenteiligem Vorgehen nahe. Eine Schülergruppe bearbeitet Anju, die andere Runu. Eine vorstrukturierte Tabelle (siehe unten) kann den Schülerinnen und Schülern ausgeteilt werden. Ein Schülerpaar pro Gruppe arbeitet auf Folie, die danach im Plenum vorgestellt wird. Die Informationen der jeweils anderen Gruppe werden in die Tabelle übertragen.

Die Besprechung von Aufgabe 5 kann als simulierte Talkshow durchgeführt werden. Um die Talkshow angemessen vorbereiten zu können, ist es nötig, dass die Schülerinnen und Schüler möglichst viele – optimalerweise alle – Meinungen ihrer Mitschüler kennen. Deshalb liegt es nahe, die Hausaufgabe auf einem gesonderten Blatt anfertigen zu lassen und im Klassenzimmer auszulegen bzw. auszuhängen (z. B. Pinwand). Die Schülerinnen und Schüler gehen umher und lesen – je nach Klassenstärke – eine bestimmte Anzahl bzw. alle Arbeiten. Im Anschluss daran kann ein kurzes Plenumsgespräch erfolgen, in dem besonders hervorstechende Haltungen kommentiert werden. Danach wird zur Talkshow übergeleitet. Diese geht insofern über die Hausaufgabe hinaus, als jetzt nicht mehr der eigene Standpunkt gefragt ist, sondern von Schülerinnen und Schülern eine Perspektivenänderung und eine Perspektivenübernahme gefordert sind. Um diese vorzubereiten bzw. zu erreichen, wurden die Standpunkte der Mitschüler in einer Lesephase zur Kenntnis genommen.

Verschiedene Rollen werden z. B. durch das Losverfahren festgelegt: ein(e) Moderator(in), verschiedene Gäste und Zuschauer, die Fragen stellen. Die Schülerinnen und Schüler bereiten die ihnen zugeloste Rolle vor, indem sie sich in einer Reflexionsphase Notizen machen. Je differenzierter die Vorgaben auf den zu ziehenden Rollenkärtchen sind, desto mehr Tiefgang verspricht die Diskussion. Mögliche Ausdifferenzierungen können erreicht werden durch folgende Angaben auf den Kärtchen:
– Geschlecht
– Alter
– Familienstand
– Kultureller Hintergrund
– Bildungsgrad
– Selbst vom Phänomen der arrangierten Ehe Betroffene(r)
– Jemand, der eine solche Ehe arrangiert hat

Solutions

Activities p. 22

1. Summarize the story in a few sentences.

In the short story extract the reader overhears two conversations: the first, on the phone between Runu, a young Indian woman living in India with her in-laws, and Anju and Sunil, a young Indian married couple living in the US; the second, between Anju and her husband. Runu and Anju have been friends since they were young girls. Now, they are both pregnant. Runu – so the amniocentesis has shown – is expecting a baby girl. Her husband and in-laws want her to abort, whereas she wants to keep the baby. In her despair she has also asked her mother for advice but has been told to do what her husband's family expect her to do. As a last resort Runu phones Anju who advises her not to accept the in-laws' order. She advises her friend to go to her own mother for help.

In the second part of the conversation, Anju and Sunil talk to each other. Anju hoped for support from Sunil, but her husband sees things from the point of view of Runu's in-laws. Anju is shocked and asks if Sunil would have wanted her to have an abortion too, if the baby she is expecting hadn't turned out to be a boy.

2. Compare Anju's and Runu's past and present situation.

	Anju	Runu
the past	The two girls played together. Anju always had changing plans for her future.	The two girls played together. Runu always wanted to have a family: a husband and many children.
the present	She lives in America with her husband. She is expecting a baby boy. She seems to be relatively independent. Her mother seems to be relatively open-minded.	She lives in India with her husband and her in-laws. She is expecting a baby girl. Her husband and her in-laws urge her to have an abortion. She is completely dependent on her husband's family.

3. Examine Sunil's position.

Sunil's position is an ambiguous one. On the one hand he seems to be a modem husband respecting the rules typical of Western civilizations. On the other hand he embodies values typical of patriarchal societies; for him it is out of the question that Runu should disobey her husband and in-laws. He totally shares the point of view of Runu's family living in India. When Anju points out his inconsequent behaviour, he reacts in an elusive way.

4. Comment on Anju's reaction to Runu's situation. In doing so, take into consideration Anju's own situation.

Anju, as an Indian woman living in America, reacts very strongly to Runu's situation. She is shocked and indignant at what is being done to her friend. By advising Runu to disobey her husband and in-laws she acts as a woman who is accustomed to living in a society where men and women have equal rights, look after themselves and are absolutely independent.

Without reflecting for a second she transposes the conditions she is living in to Runu whose life, however, is determined by different parameters. She seems to forget that her advice can't be transposed to a society with very different rules and values. Her anger, indignation and abomination can be understood because of the fact that she is Runu's friend. She applies behaviour which is valid in America to Indian rules and values and these are incompatible. Anju does not realize what she is doing. Although her reaction can very well be understood on a human level and, especially on a woman-to-woman level, it is doubtful whether she gives her friend suitable advice.

5. What is your personal opinion about arranged marriages? Write a short comment.

In some societies arranged marriages are part of the cultural tradition and have been practised for a long time. Parents choose the future partner for their son or daughter, make arrangements with the parents of the future partner and arrange the wedding ceremony. Very often the couple only meets the day when they get married. Love or personal inclination don't play a prominent part in this procedure. It is social, religious, financial and cultural reasons that are decisive.

Personal happiness is left behind. In our Western society where the pursuit of personal happiness, freedom and independence are so important, an arranged marriage is hardly acceptable. Having to spend the rest of your life with someone you don't love is a nightmare!

Interpreter of Maladies

Jhumpa Lahiri

Author and text Jhumpa Lahiri was born in London in 1967 to Indian parents. She was brought up in South Kingstown, Rhode Island, America. As her mother wanted to raise her children to be Indian, Jhumpa learned about her Bengali heritage from an early age. She graduated from South Kingstown High School and later received her BA in English literature from Barnard College in 1989. She then received multiple degrees from Boston University: an MA in English, an MA in Creative Writing, an MA in Comparative Literature and a PhD in Renaissance Studies. She took up a fellowship at Princetown's Fine Arts Work Center which lasted until 1998. In 2000 she was awarded the Pulitzer Prize for Fiction. In 2001 she married Alberto Vourvoulias-Bush, a journalist. Lahiri currently lives in Brooklyn with her husband and two children. She has been a Vice President of the PEN American Center since 2005. Her stories deal with the lives of Indians in exile, of people torn between traditional Indian customs and those of the Western world.

The excerpt from the short story *The Interpreter of Maladies* gives an insight into the life of a newly-wed Indian couple. The marriage between the narrator and his wife Mala had been arranged by the narrator's family. Unlike Mala who had been living in India so far, the narrator is a lecturer at MIT and is used to living in a large American city. The excerpt reveals the couple's different way of living and their way of gradually getting used to each other in spite of the cultural differences that separate them.

Unterrichtsempfehlungen

Falls die Talkshow beim Text „Arranged Marriage" durchgeführt wurde, kann zusätzlich zur Einstiegsaufgabe auf S. 23 im Schülerbuch wiederholt werden, wie sich Männer im Rollenspiel zur arrangierten Ehe geäußert haben.

Zur Erklärung des Konzepts „culture clash" beraten sich die Schülerinnen und Schüler in Vierergruppen in buzz groups. Sie wählen eine(n) Sprecher(in), der/die ihre Ergebnisse den anderen im Plenum vorstellt. Dabei arbeiten sie mit zuvor ausgeteilten Moderationskärtchen, die sie an der Tafel um das Konzept „culture clash" positionieren. Nach der schriftlichen Bearbeitung von Aufgabe 2 werden die Schülerinnen und Schüler aufgefordert, aus Zeitschriften (oder anderen Quellen, z. B. dem Internet) Bilder von Frauen mitzubringen, die ihrer Meinung nach Mala sein könnten und begründen ihre Wahl. Falls sie kein geeignetes Bild finden, bringen sie eine „unpassende" Abbildung mit und begründen wiederum.

Um Empathiefähigkeit zu fördern, versetzen sich die Schülerinnen und Schüler zur Bearbeitung der Aufgabe 5 nach der schriftlichen Bearbeitung der Aufgabe in die Situation Malas und überlegen, wie sie sich an ihrer Stelle fühlten und was sie tun würden. Sie vervollständigen mindestens drei Sätze, die beginnen mit „If I were Mala ..."

Damit möglichst viele Ergebnisse (Briefe) aus Aufgabe 6 gelesen werden können, kann eine „Lesestunde" abgehalten werden. Da lautes Vorlesen nach kurzer Zeit die Aufmerksamkeit der Zuhörerschaft überfordert, werden alle Briefe eingesammelt und neu verteilt. Die Schülerinnen und Schüler tauschen die Texte nach Lektüre untereinander aus; je nach Gruppenstärke werden alle oder eine zuvor festgelegte Mindestanzahl an Briefen gelesen. Danach erfolgt ein Gedankenaustausch im Plenum.

Solutions

Explain the concept of *culture clash*.
Before you read p. 23
— Representatives of different cultures meet in the same place; their different habits and customs are not compatible with each other.
— Lack of understanding for the other culture
— Feeling of strangeness/estrangement

1. Describe the male protagonist's attitude towards his arranged marriage. To what extent is it reflected in his behaviour towards Mala?
Activities p. 25
The male protagonist has a rather indifferent attitude towards his marriage. He is neither happy nor sad about the fact that he is to marry a woman chosen by his family. He considers marriage as a duty, something that is inevitable. It is a duty he has to fulfil just as all the other men in the world. Marriage, for him, has nothing to do with emotions. This attitude is reflected in the male protagonist's way of treating his wife. Although he sees and knows that she is unhappy because she is missing her parents, he doesn't do anything in order to make her feel better. Her sadness is, for him, just as inevitable as the fact that he is getting married to her.

2. What kind of woman is Mala?
Mala is a 27-year-old Indian woman. As she has relatively dark skin, many men have already rejected marrying her. She is the only child of a Beleghato school teacher and his wife. Mala is able to do various household tasks (e. g. cooking, knitting, embroidery) and she can draw landscapes and recite poems by Tagore. She seems to be a shy, silent woman who accepts doing the things she is told to do.

3. Analyse their relationship in India. How does it develop in America?
Their relationship in India seems to be distant. None of them seems to know what the other expects and they seem to be unable to talk to each other. They are each engaged in separate activities (he is reading a guide book, she is doing her toilet), they seem to be living side by side rather than together with each other.
In America things don't really change as far as the narrator is concerned. Before Mala comes to America he is still very distant and not interested in her arrival. The fact that he will be reunited with his wife doesn't arouse any emotions in him. But gradually he becomes aware of the fact that things will change. He grows more attentive (i. e. when he sees another Indian woman struggling with her sari when a dog barks at her), but still he doesn't show emotions. He knows that it is his duty to look after Mala and to protect her, but he only does so because he has to. When Mala finally arrives in America he doesn't even touch or kiss her when they meet at the airport. Nor has he got a welcome present for her.
With Mala, things are different. Whereas she seemed rather passive and withdrawn in India, she gives the impression of being more lively and determined in America. She obviously has accepted her new role as a housewife. She cooks, cleans the apartment and tidies things. But the quality of their relationship still remains distant and emotionless.

4. Discuss the male protagonist's view of himself as a husband.
The male protagonist sees his role as a husband as a duty every man has to fulfil. He hasn't chosen his wife by himself but had her chosen by his family. He doesn't show any emotions towards her. He knows that he is responsible for her and that he has to take care of her. He does what has to be done but all in all, he is very reluctant.

5. Reflect on Mala's situation.

Mala is a young Indian woman who has recently come to America where her husband lives. She has never been to America before and isn't used to the country, nor to using the English language. Apart from her husband, who is at work all day long at MIT, she doesn't know anyone. She spends her time alone in the house doing housework. She hasn't got a job, so she is completely dependent on her husband. The only contact she has apart from her husband is with her parents in India to whom she often writes letters.

6. Mala often writes letters to her family in India telling them about her new life in America. Put yourself in her shoes and write a letter to her family in India.

Dear family,

I hope you are all fine. So am I. My new life as a housewife isn't very exciting. I do all the housework: cooking, cleaning and tidying up. My husband isn't in very often and I feel rather lonely. I miss you so much!!! In order to have a little bit of India here in this cold country I keep up Indian traditions as much as I can. My husband, however, has already adopted much of the American way of life – he eats cereal in the morning for breakfast and not rice, as most Bengali husbands do. So I think it's my duty to keep up our traditional way of life. That's why I often prepare Indian meals like chicken curry with fresh garlic and ginger, just the way we used to eat it at home in Beleghata. You just can't imagine how much I miss you!!!
Every time I go into our bathroom and smell the Pearl soap I bought in the Indian shop around the corner it almost makes me cry! Anyway, my husband is a real scholar – his household isn't well equipped. Just imagine, he didn't have a potato peeler! Nor did he have a tablecloth! I asked him for money to buy these things and he gave me the money, but was not pleased that I had asked him to. But what else can I do? On the other hand, if we don't spend all the money he earns, hopefully we can fly to India soon. I miss you ever so much!!!

Love, Mala

India's New Worldly Women

Pete Engardio

Author and text   Pete Engardio is a senior writer at *Business Week*. He was the magazine's Asia correspondent for six years and is co-author of the book „Meltdown: Asia's Boom, Bust and Beyond" published in 2000. He has won numerous major awards for his coverage of global issues.
American TV has had an enormous influence on younger Indian women. Traditional values such as submissiveness and frugality are getting lost according to two studies carried out by Grey Global Group. The new trend among Indian women is quite different: they want more freedom and individualism, their career is important to them, and arranged marriages are rejected. The young Indian women's outlook on life is perceived as revolutionary by Indian society.

Unterrichtsempfehlungen

Als vorbereitender Einstieg informieren sich die Schülerinnen und Schüler darüber, welche Lebenspläne junge, moderne Frauen haben. Besonders für die männlichen

Schüler beinhaltet diese Aufgabe einen Perspektivenwechsel. Unter Zuhilfenahme von Stichwortkärtchen berichten sie im Plenum.

Aufgabe 2 eignet sich zur Bearbeitung in arbeitsteiliger Gruppenarbeit. Die Schülerinnen und Schüler füllen eine vorstrukturierte Tabelle aus. Ein Schüler pro Gruppe arbeitet auf Folie, die später als Ergebnissicherung für alle dient. Ein anderes Gruppenmitglied trägt die Ergebnisse vor, die jeweils andere Gruppe überträgt die Informationen in die Tabelle.

Zur Lösung von Aufgabe 4 denken die Schülerinnen und Schüler zunächst allein über die Fragestellung nach. Danach finden sie sich in Vierergruppen zusammmen, um ein *place mat* auszufüllen. Sie notieren ihre eben gemachten Gedanken in jeweils einer Ecke des *place mats*, danach lesen sie die Notizen der anderen drei Mitschüler und diskutieren darüber. Sie einigen sich nach der Diskussion auf ein *statement*, das sie in die Mitte des *place mats* als gemeinsamen Konsens schreiben.

Ein von der Lehrkraft vorbereiteter DIN A3-Bogen, der wie folgt aufgeteilt werden kann, stellt das *place mat* dar.

	Schüler 1	
Schüler 2	gemeinsames Statement	Schüler 4
	Schüler 3	

Solutions

1. **Describe how American TV has affected Indian women's lives.**

Activities p. 27

   American TV has had a deep and crucial impact on the lives of young Indian women. New trends unknown to them before began to influence them and effectively changed their lives.

2. **Contrast the traditional lifestyle and the modern lifestyle of Indian women.**
   Ein mögliches Tafelbild kann wie folgt aussehen:

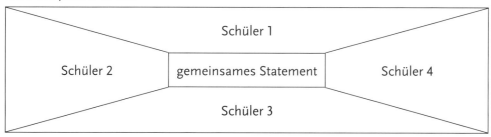

traditional lifestyle of Indian women	modern lifestyle of Indian women
– They do what their parents and husbands tell them to do.	– They believe in financial independence.
– They don't spend much money but rather try to make the best use of scarce resources.	– Arranged marriages are not wanted any more. Indian women wish to decide by themselves if and whom they are going to marry.
– They are modest.	– Finding good jobs and having a glamorous career is extremely important for them.

3. **Sum up the trends influencing young Indian women.**
   The trends influencing young Indian women are personal and marital freedom, the creation of an individual style, jobs and career, and modern relationships in which men have to take their share of household chores.

4. Evaluate these trends from your European point of view.

Seen from a European point of view, these trends are anything but revolutionary. They are standard and conceived as being absolutely normal.

For a European, the idea of having one's husband chosen by the family and of being forced to do what parents and husband say is completely inconceivable. So is the idea that women stay at home, doing all the housework and looking after the children while the male partner earns the money – and has the last word! For Europeans, traditional Indian values are hard to understand as well as the fact that women were willing to accept these strict rules until now. What is perceived as a revolution by Indian society is seen as backwardness by Europeans.

Boom Times

Why India's Hot ... How It's Changing

This double page gives an overview on modern India's economic and social reality. It shows how India is changing from a traditional Asian country to a western-style profit-orientated market economy.

Author and text

Unterrichtsempfehlungen

Als Einstimmung auf das Thema „Indiens Wirtschaft" erhalten die Schülerinnen und Schüler den Auftrag, die Doppelseite im Buch zu lesen und die Bereiche (*economy, society*) zu bestimmen, aus denen die Beispiele für den wirtschaftlichen Aufstieg Indiens entnommen sind. Diese werden an der Tafel mit den angegebenen Beispielen illustriert und dienen als Grundlage für die anschließende Diskussion im Plenum, in der die Schülerinnen und Schüler die wirtschaftliche und soziale Entwicklung Indiens kommentieren sollen. Dabei sollte deutlich werden, dass Indiens Aufstieg zur Wirtschaftsmacht Indiens Gesellschaft nachhaltig verändert bzw. modernisiert. Das Tafelbild wird am Ende der Diskussion um dieses Resümée ergänzt.

The „New India"

Economy
- young, skilled, English-speaking workforce
- preferred place for call centres where English is spoken
- attractive outsourcing location for foreign investors (e. g. BMW, Cisco, Nokia)
- preferred location for the services industry (IT, finance, R & D)
- Indian companies like Infosys, Wipro and Tata have become global players.
- Apart from traditional industry, Indian agriculture is also growing and preparing to compete on the international market.

Society
- Young people who work in Indian industry no longer adhere to traditional value systems.
- More women are getting divorced or staying single.
- Premarital sex is becoming more accepted.
- Young people are earning money which they love to spend.
- Western lifestyle (e. g. MacDonald's, Benetton, luxury goods, mobile phones, travel) is conquering Indian society.

India's booming economy changes India's traditional society.

Folgende Internetadressen geben umfassende Auskunft über die Aktivitäten deutscher Firmen in Indien (Aufgabe 2):

http://www.indiadaily.com/editorial/4974.asp
http://www.ibef.org ➜ Search: „germany"
http://www.ieo.org/kav002.html
http://www.young-germany.de ➜ Search: „india special"

Zur Bearbeitung von Aufgabe 3 diskutieren die Schülerinnen und Schüler die Frage in Kleingruppen zu höchstens 6 Teilnehmern und schreiben die Ergebnisse ihrer Diskussion auf verschiedenfarbige (*possibilities – dangers*) Moderationskarten. Die Anzahl der Karten, die jeder Gruppe zur Verfügung steht, sollte je nach Klassenstärke so limitiert werden, dass insgesamt nicht mehr als 20 Stichpunkte verzeichnet werden. Diese werden an der Tafel bzw. Moderationswand gesammelt und optimiert, d. h. gleiche oder ähnliche Aspekte werden aussortiert. Der so entstandene Ideenspeicher wird von den Schülerinnen und Schülern übernommen und dient als Grundlage einer schriftlichen Ausarbeitung, die als Hausaufgabe erledigt werden kann.

Die folgende Auswahl an Aspekten erhebt keinen Anspruch auf Vollständigkeit.

Modern India

possibilities	dangers
– prosperous society	– loss of traditional values
– money for schools, hospitals, etc.	– emphasis of money and free market principles
– possibility of creating a just society	– consumerism
– modern lifestyle and easier life for all	– further discrimination of society into rich and poor

Die in dem zur Diskussion stehenden Artikel angesprochenen Inhalte lassen sich grob in zwei Themenblöcke, Wirtschaft und gesellschaftliches Leben, einteilen. Während sich ersterer mit der momentanen Situation der indischen Wirtschaft und hier schwerpunktmäßig mit ausländischen Investoren in Indien beschäftigt, konzentriert sich letzterer auf die zunehmende Verwestlichung bestimmter Schichten der indischen Gesellschaft.

Als Informationsquelle für die in Aufgabe 4 geforderte Präsentation können für den Themenblock „Wirtschaft" neben den Informationen im Schülerbuch die oben aufgelisteten Internetadressen benutzt werden. Einen Überblick über „lifestyle in India" bietet u. a. www.indianetzone.com bzw. das Kapitel „Bollywood" im Schülerband.

Solutions

Activities p. 30

1. Use the information given on the two pages above to comment on the "new India" emerging at the beginning of the 21st century.
Individual answers

2. The text mentions BMW among the foreign investors in India. Search the Internet for information on other German companies investing in India. Enter keywords like "German investment in India" or "German companies in India" in a search engine.
Individual answers

3. Discuss the positive and negative aspects of this development in class. What are the possibilities, what are the dangers?
Possibilities and dangers in modern India
Modern India, as we see it developing at the moment, offers a lot of chances for Indian society, but also poses some serious dangers.
For many reasons India is a very attractive country for foreign investors like BMW or Nokia who find well-trained personnel who are ready to work for modest wages and who speak the global language, English.
A booming industry also means a high level of tax income from industry and private persons, which the state can use for the creation or improvement of educational and health-care systems. A better education will give more people the chance to get well-paid jobs and so life will change for the better for many people.
On the other hand rapid modernization of Indian society can also become very dangerous to Indian culture and traditions which are likely to be given up for the blessings of modern consumerism. If money is the prevalent value in a society, it will be

further, and more radically, divided into „haves" and „havenots", into wealthy and poor people, and the latter will hardly have any chance of changing their situation. So the transition from a largely rural society to a modern market economy should be made slowly and carefully, and politics should accompany this process with appropriate measures to make sure that the „new India" offers the chance of a better life for the whole of its society.

4. Work in groups. Choose one of the areas mentioned in the survey above and get more information on it. Prepare a presentation on your subject.
Creative task

India's IT industry: Dream Run

The text deals with India's rise to an economic superpower whose success is based on the country's IT software and services industry. According to the text, the secret of India's economic success is, on the one hand, a favourable government policy which supports foreign and Indian companies by providing the necessary infrastructure and a favourable legal framework. On the other hand, Indian colleges and universities educate a highly qualified workforce for the country's booming IT industry.

Author and text

Unterrichtsempfehlungen

Da Schülerinnen und Schüler oft nur über unzureichende Kenntnisse rhetorischer Figuren verfügen, erscheint es vor der Bearbeitung von Aufgabe 4 sinnvoll, der eigentlichen Bearbeitung der Aufgabe eine kurze Erarbeitungsphase vorzuschalten, in der die wichtigsten Stilfiguren gesammelt und definiert werden.

- metaphor: a word or phrase used to describe an object or an action which has similar qualities but which it does not literally denote; a poetical comparison without "as" or "like"
- simile: a comparison introduced by "as" or "like"
- rhetorical question: a question to which no answer is required or expected
- personification: an attribution of human characteristics to things or ideas

Die im Unterrichtsgespräch erarbeiteten Definitionen werden zusammen mit Beispielen aus dem Text und den entsprechenden Erläuterungen in die vorgegebene Tabelle (Worksheet 3) eingetragen.

Aufgabe 5 kann in Kleingruppen erledigt werden, wobei sich je zwei Schülerinnen und Schüler mit Begriffen aus dem Bereich „companies", „global market" sowie „employees" und „products" (die beiden letzteren können zusammengefasst werden, da sich hierfür weniger Begriffe im Text finden) beschäftigen. Die Untergruppen sammeln zunächst Begriffe zu ihrem Thema und organisieren sie dann in einer eigenen Mind-map. Die vier „Teilmindmaps" werden dann zu einer Gesamtdarstellung zusammengefasst. Die Gruppenergebnisse können über Overheadfolie präsentiert, gegebenenfalls korrigiert und dann für die Lerngruppe kopiert werden. Die Erstellung einer englisch-deutschen Vokabelliste zum Thema kann in die Hausaufgabe verlegt werden. Um das erarbeitete Vokabular umzusetzen können die Schülerinnen und Schüler zusätzlich aufgefordert werden, Sätze zu bilden.
Die unten stehende ungeordnete Wortliste sowie alle weiteren Lösungsvorschläge zu dieser Aufgabe erheben keinen Anspruch auf Vollständigkeit.

NASSCOM (National Association of Software and Service Companies) ist sowohl die indische Handelskammer für die IT- und Serviceindustrie als auch ein internationaler Zusammenschluss von insgesamt 1100 Firmen, darunter 250 internationalen Konzernen aus den USA, Europa, Japan und China, der es sich zum Ziel gesetzt hat, die Software-Forschung und Entwicklung sowie deren Vermarktung mit dem Ziel voranzutreiben, Indien im 21. Jahrhundert als führende Nation in der Informationstechnologie zu etablieren.

Die unter Aufgabe 6 angegebene Internetadresse bietet umfangreiche Informationen zu NASSCOM selbst und zu ihren Aktivitäten im nationalen und internationalen Bereich. Folgende Themen sind für eine Erarbeitung und Präsentation in Kleingruppen denkbar:

NASSCOM as a national and international organization

national and international NASSCOM members

NASSCOM policy

NASSOM forums

NASSCOM's importance in Indian society and economy

Solutions

Before you read p. 30

Describe this photo. What its message?

The photo shows a man sleeping on a makeshift bed under a lorry. He is probably the lorry driver, who is either too poor to own a house, or to be able to pay for a room in a motel on his tours. Above the sleeping man we see the slogan „India is great", which refers to the booming IT industry in India and is in stark contrast to the man's situation. The lorry was produced by TATA group, one of the most important companies in India.

The photo shows that only a small part of Indian society reaps the benefits of the county's IT boom, while others are completely untouched by it.

Activities p. 32

1. Explain why companies from all over the world are turning to India for help in the IT services sectors.

Foreign companies turn to India because they find experts for old and new technologies there in all the areas that are required; there is a large number of highly skilled workers.

2. What role are politicians playing in India's IT boom?

The government of Karnataka, the centre of Indian IT industry, supports its IT industry with the necessary telecommunication and policy infrastructure and makes it easy for local companies to start businesses or expand them by offering financial and administrative help. It also provides the necessary financial and political basis for foreign companies to invest in Karnataka.

3. Comment on the job prospects of Indian IT engineers.

Although India has a large amount of trained software engineers (about 75,000 graduate per year) they are all offered good jobs at home and abroad. When they decide to go abroad, most of them work for US companies, but a large number also join companies in the EU where there were 1.6 million vacancies for IT engineers in 2003, with Germany alone offering 400,000 jobs.

4. Identify and explain the figures of speech used in the text.

	metaphor	simile	rhetorical question	personification
definition	a word or phrase used to describe an object or an action which has similar qualities but which it does not literally denote	a comparison introduced by "as" or "like"	a question to which no answer is expected or required	an attribution of human characteristics to things or ideas
example	... as the spearhead of India's export attack. (l. 3) ...the Indian software engine (l. 11) ... their playing ground? (l. 16)	Like old wine ... (l. 4)	What is it then that has enabled Indian software companies to make the global market their playing ground? (ll. 15 f.)	...the Indian software and services industry has matured, become more refined and moved up the value chain ... (ll. 4 ff.) India stands tall today among global contemporaries in the software market, ... (ll. 19 ff.)
function in the text	Metaphors illustrate the argument of a text by linking it with a different context. They are very effective because the reader or listener has to decipher the linking elements.	Similes illustrate the argument of a text by comparing it with elements from a different context.	Rhetorical questions emphasize the argument of a text and, in addition, create a dramatic effect, which is why they are often used in speeches.	Personifications emphasize the argument of a text and make it more vivid.

5. Make a list of expressions related to the IT industry that are used in the text and arrange them in a mind-map. Look up their German meaning.

companies	global market	employees	products
– software and services industry (l. 2) – customer (l. 6) – corporate (l. 7) – software needs (l. 8) – expertise (l. 10) – technology (l. 10) – vendor (l. 21) – state-of-the-art facility (l. 31) – software sector (l. 32) – to set up shop (. 37) – software and services marketplace (l. 39) – hardware and software industry (ll. 43 ff.) – training center (l. 45) – end-user organization (l. 52 f.)	– global economic slow-down (l. 1) – steady pace of growth (l. 2) – export attack (l. 3) – global customer (l. 14) – software market (l. 19 f.) – World Bank-funded study (l. 21) – outsourcing (l. 22) – average growth rate (l. 26) – software development activity (ll. 26 f.) – boost (l. 34)	– skilled manpower (l. 12 f.) – PhD (l. 13) – computer science graduate (l. 13) – software professional (l. 50) – software engineer (l. 51) – newly qualified personnel (l. 54)	– value chain (l. 5) – legacy and new technology solution (l. 9)

Mind-map

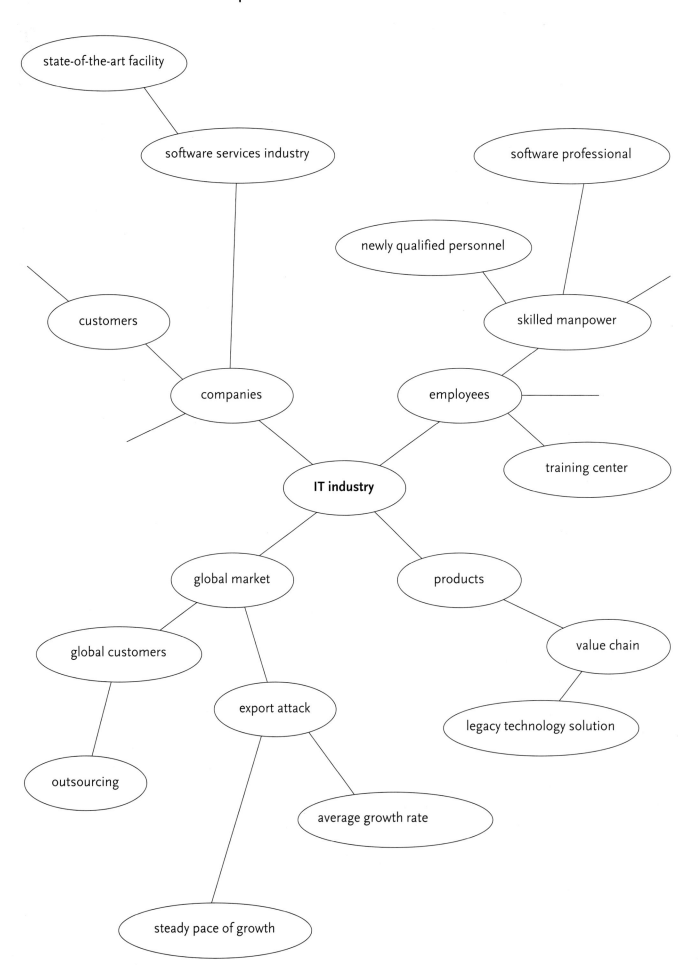

IT industry: word-list English – German

– average growth rate	durchschnittliche Wachstumsrate
– boost	Zunahme
– computer science graduate	Absolvent eines Informatikstudiums
– corporate	Unternehmen
– customer	Kunde
– end-user organization	Endverbraucherorganisation
– expertise	Fachwissen
– export attack	Exportangriff
– global customer	internationale, weltweite Kundschaft
– global economic slowdown	weltweiter wirtschaftlicher Rückgang
– hardware and software industry	Hardware- und Software-Industrie
– legacy and new technology solution	Lösung, die auf hergebrachten und auf neuen Technologien beruht
– newly qualified personnel	neu qualifiziertes Personal
– outsourcing	Outsourcing, Verlagerung von Produktionszweigen in Billiglohnländer
– PhD	Doktorwürde, Doktortitel
– to set up shop	ein Geschäft, eine Firma eröffnen
– skilled manpower	qualifiziertes Personal
– software and services industry	Software- und Serviceindustrie
– software and services marketplace	Software- und Servicemarkt
– software development activity	Tätigkeit im Bereich von Softwareentwicklung
– software engineer	Software-Ingenieur, Programmierer
– software market	Softwaremarkt
– software needs	Anforderungen, Wünsche, Bedarf im Softwarebereich
– software professional	Arbeitnehmer mit einer Qualifikation, Ausbildung im Softwarebereich
– software sector	Softwarebereich
– state-of-the-art facility	Einrichtung auf dem höchsten Entwicklungsniveau
– steady pace of growth	gleichmäßiges Wachstum
– technology	Technologie
– training center	Ausbildungszentrum
– value chain	hier: Stellenwert
– vendor	Verkäufer
– World Bank-funded study	eine von der Weltbank finanzierte Studie

6. Search the Internet for information on NASSCOM and give a short NASSCOM presentation. Activities p. 33

Creative task

7. Analyze the statistics below and use your results to write a short text.

The three statistics underline the success the Indian software and services industry has had since the year 2000.

While the growth rate of India's software and services industry has remained below the 10 percent mark up to the year 2000/2001, it will have grown by 87 percent by the year 2008. A similar development is shown in the graph for software exports which grew by 25 percent in only one year (between 2001/2002 and 2002/2003). This clearly shows that India's IT industry relies and depends on foreign markets. India is especially suited for competing on the global market because its IT workforce is highly qualified and speaks the number one global language, English.

These statistics show that India is well underway to reach the very top of the international IT market.

Worksheet 3

Figures of Speech

Fill in the definitions of the figures of speech, then look for examples from the text and explain their function.

	metaphor	simile	rhetorical question	personification
definition				
example				
function in the text				

Green Profits

Ron Moreau/Sudip Mazumdar

Ron Moreau and Supip Mazumdar work for *Newsweek Magazine*.
Green Profits explains the growing interest of Indian industrial conglomerates in so-far
neglected Indian agriculture. Indian industry has come to see Indian agriculture as a
profitable future market for their own goods, and therefore invests in new technologies
and equipment for farming. With these investments, India's industrial giants hope to
increase farm yields which can be sold on the Asian and even international markets. If
farmers sell their goods at higher prices, they will have more money at their disposal,
and will themselves form a market for India's high-tech products.

Author and text

Unterrichtsempfehlungen

Die Bearbeitung von Aufgabe 4 kann als Partnerarbeit konzipiert werden. Partner I erhält den Auftrag, die im Text beschriebene gegenwärtige Situation der indischen Land-
wirtschaft zu untersuchen, Partner II soll sich mit ihren Zukunftsprognosen beschäftigen. Im Anschluss an die Partnerarbeit tauschen jeweils drei Paare ihre Ergebnisse aus
und übernehmen sie in Tabellenform ins Heft. Dieser Heftaufschrieb kann als Grundlage einer schriftlichen Ausarbeitung in der Hausaufgabe dienen.

Rural India

Present situation	Prospects for the future
– bad infrastructure	– increase of farmers' yields
– poverty	– improvement of food processing and export operations
– small, unproductive farms	– increase in farmers' wealth
– government policy slows down development.	– new markets in the Middle East and Europe
↓	↓
660 million Indians live in poverty ...	... but are India's biggest future market.

Aufgabe 6 kann als eine die Beschäftigung mit dem Text abschließende Gruppenarbeit
gestaltet werden, in der die Schülerinnen und Schüler die Ergebnisse ihrer Beschäftigung mit dem Text kreativ verarbeiten können. Um nicht nur eine inhaltliche, sondern
auch eine sprachliche Umsetzung sicherzustellen, sollte bei der Aufgabenstellung dar-
auf hingewiesen werden, dass die Handzettel oder Poster mindestens eine Textzeile
bzw. einen Slogan enthalten müssen.

Solutions

What do these pictures tell you about the current situation of agriculture in India?
Agriculture in India seems to be on the threshold of a new age. While a great part of
Indian farming still relies mainly on manual labour, computer technology is slowly find-
ing its way into agriculture, revolutionizing production and marketing processes.

Before you read p. 34

1. Sum up the general ideas of the text in a short oral statement.
Both Indian industry and the Indian government are trying to reform the Indian agricultural sector. Big Indian companies are sponsoring computer equipment for Indian farmers so that they can use the Internet to get information on the weather,

Activities p. 36

modern technologies and food prices. They are doing so because they see a big market in the Indian agricultural sector. The government is supporting Indian farmers by giving up old socialist-style systems of subsidies and strict regulations of the agricultural market. They are also introducing tax reforms and supporting investors who are willing to put money into agriculture because they see the Indian agricultural sector as a huge resource which has not been tapped so far.

2. **Why are India's farmers becoming more attractive for companies like ITC?**
Companies which are not involved in agriculture at all invest in it mainly for two reasons. First, they make profit from the goods which are produced on farms. For example ITC, a tobacco, food and hotel corporation, can sell farm products to customers directly, or use them in their hotel catering systems.
Second, if Indian farmers increase their production and are financially better off, they will be willing to spend money and so form a huge potential market for the goods which are produced by these companies.

3. **In which ways are politicians supporting the modernization of India's agricultural sector?**
The Indian government provides financial support for farmers, for example by introducing tax holidays. It helps to develop the countryside by building roads, modernizing the infrastructure or improving production conditions. The government also introduced reforms which make investment in the rural sector more attractive and which lift old market restrictions for agricultural goods.

4. **Contrast the present situation of rural India and its prospects for the future as envisaged by ITC.**
Rural India – problems and chances
The present situation of Indian farmers is rather desperate. Farmwork is mainly done without the help of machines. Manual labour predominates. This means growing methods are old-fashioned and unproductive. A bad infrastructure and laws restricting, rather than regulating, the trade of farm goods add to this difficult situation. So the 660 million Indians who live in rural India and work in agriculture live in great poverty.
If the reforms envisaged by companies like ITC can be carried out successfully, the situation for Indian farmers will change for the better. The introduction of modern computer equipment, which helps farmers to improve and modernize growing processes, may finally lead to increased yields and this would mean that Indian farmers could serve greater markets at home and abroad. They may have the chance to live wealthier and more secure lives in the near future.

5. **What devices does the author use to make his text convincing?**
To make his text more convincing the author uses
   - examples from real life: farmer Amar Singh Verma (l. 2 f.)
   - names of politicians currently in power: Prime Minister Manmohan Singh (l. 46)
   - numbers and statistics: 50 % increase (l. 9 f.)

         ITC, a $ 7.5 billion tobacco, food and hotel corporation (l. 14)
         660 million Indians live off the land (l. 25 f.)
         the sector accounts for 21 % of India's GDP (l. 26 f.)

6. **Design an advert or a leaflet as an ITC public relations person to convince farmers to join your project.**
Possible slogans:
   - Modern farms for modern India
   - ITC paves the way into your future
   - Invest in modern technology – invest in the future

Poverty and Despair

While the previous text deals with positive prospects for the future of Indian agriculture, this short informative text with pictures shows the sad reality in many rural areas in India where farmers still rely on old-fashioned growing methods which do not provide enough income to sustain their families. Some of them see suicide as the only way out of this situation because it entitles their families to financial compensation by the state.

Author and text

Unterrichtsempfehlungen

Die Ergebnisse der Gruppenarbeit bei Aufgabe 1 können dem Plenum entweder über Overheadfolie präsentiert und im Anschluss daran für die Klasse kopiert oder auf Postern im Klassenzimmer ausgehängt und im Rahmen eines Museumsgangs erläutert werden. Inhaltlich sollte in den graphischen Darstellungen eine Kausalkette deutlich werden.

Vor der Bearbeitung von Aufgabe 2 sollten die Schülerinnen und Schüler mit den Grundzügen des Aufbaus der klassischen Rede vertraut gemacht werden. Dies kann mithilfe eines Tafelanschriebs geschehen.

The classical speech

1. introduction (exordium): the introduction attracts the audience's interest
2. statement of the case (narratio): information on the subject of the speech
3. argument (argumentatio): explanation of the argument
                    a. proof of the case (confirmatio)
                    b. refutation of possible opposing arguments (refutatio)
4. conclusion (peroratio): summary and appeal to the audience

Im Anschluss an diese Einführung sammeln die Schülerinnen und Schüler in Partnerarbeit Ideen für die Rede und tragen diese stichwortartig in die entsprechenden Zeilen des Arbeitsblatts (Worksheet 4) ein. Die schriftliche Ausarbeitung der Rede erfolgt in der Hausaufgabe, die dann in der Folgestunde im Hinblick auf die Aufgabenstellung diskutiert wird.

Solutions

Activities p. 37

1. **Get together in small groups and discuss the situation of Indian farmers in terms of cause and effect. Then present the results of your discussion in a graph.**

   The crisis of Indian agriculture

   soil is damaged by too much fertilizer
   or pesticides or by lack of rain
   ↓

   farmers' profits are ruined
   ↓

   farmers cannot afford seeds or fertilizers
   ↓

   farmers earn even less
   ↓

   farmers have to borrow money
   ↓

   farmers cannot pay back their loans
   ↓

   farmers lose their farms
   ↓

   farmers do not earn anything
   ↓

   farmers commit suicide for compensation money

2. **You are a progressive member of the Indian parliament. Use the information from the two texts on agriculture to write a speech to convince politicians to help the agricultural sector by lifting restrictions and adopting free market principles. Read your speeches in class, then discuss the different approaches.**

   Writing a classical speech

classical speech	The future of Indian agriculture
1. introduction	– the situation of Indian agriculture – industry's interest in agriculture – future possibilities for Indian agriculture
2. statement of the case	living and working on Indian farms: – no technical equipment – manual labour – traditional ways of production – Farmers are not trained in modern farming. – Farmers are too poor to invest or modernize. – Many farmers commit suicide to ensure financial compensation for their families.
3. argument	Indian agriculture has to be modernized: – Indian agriculture and the Indian IT industry have to work together. – Every Indian farmer should have access to the Internet. – Solar energy should be used to create electricity. – The government should make it attractive for industry to invest in agriculture (tax holidays or subsidies for potential investors). – The government should enable farmers to invest (cheap loans). – The government should improve the infrastructure and irrigation systems.

4. conclusion	Everyone has to be active in order to improve the situation of Indian agriculture: – Farmers have to be willing to modernize farming. – Industry has to be ready to invest in farming. – The government should support both groups.

The future of Indian agriculture

Ladies and Gentlemen,

The situation of Indian agriculture has long been neglected by the government and society. Only recently have companies like ITC, Tata or Bhati Group brought the ailing Indian agricultural sector into the focus of public interest by singling it out as a profitable field for investment. Let me first give you an impression of what living and working on a farm is like for many Indians. Indian farming today does largely without any technical support. You will find hardly any machines on Indian fields. Manual labour is still the basis of Indian farming today. Crops are grown the way they were grown by our forefathers and there is hardly any knowledge of modern irrigation or fertilization methods.

If fertilizers are used at all, then without any expertise, which does more harm than good in many cases because the soil can be made infertile.

Farmers do not have the means to modernize their farms because they are too poor to invest. Some of them turn to banks, or worse, to money lenders for help and usually cannot pay the high interest rates. This means they will sooner or later lose their farms and sink even lower into poverty, living desperate lives in the slums of India's big cities.

Farmers in our country are so desperate that committing suicide is often their last means to guarantee the survival of their families, at least for some time, as their deaths entitle their families to financial compensation from the state.

There is, however, a way out of all this, if we pursue the policy of modernizing Indian agriculture introduced by some of the main industrial companies.

It is vital that Indian agriculture and Indian IT technology should be brought together if Indian agriculture is to succeed on the international market. Every Indian farmer should have access to the Internet, either in his private house or at least in a community centre in his village as the Internet provides important information on modern growing technologies, the weather and prices on the international food market.

Many parts of rural India still have no electricity to run computers, but alternative energy like sunlight can be used with the help of solar panels so that every farmer could create his own energy.

But modernizing agricultural production is not everything. Farmers usually cannot afford to buy IT equipment. So it should be made attractive for companies to invest in the rural sector. This means that the government has to grant tax holidays or subsidies for those companies which are willing to assist Indian farmers on their way into the 21st century. Politicians also have to lift restrictions imposed on agriculture, and open the food market to the rules and laws of a modern market economy. Furthermore, the government should give farmers loans to invest in their own businesses, and improve the infrastructure and irrigation systems.

Ladies and gentleman, as you can see, there is a lot to do for each one of us.

Indian farmers have to be willing to change their traditional ways of farming, Indian industry has to be willing to invest in farming and Indian politicians have to be ready to support both groups in as many ways as possible. If we all work together we can achieve the major objective of bringing Indian agriculture to the very top and making this another Indian success story.

Worksheet 4

Writing a Classical Speech

Work with your partner and collect ideas for a classical speech then fill in the grid.

classical speech	The future of Indian agriculture
1. introduction	
2. statement of the case	
3. argument	
4. conclusion	

Klausur

Bangalore: High-tech's New Hub

Thomas L. Friedman

Bangalore, India – Every time I visit India, Indians always ask me to compare India with China. Lately, I have responded like this: If India and China were both highways, the Chinese highway would be a six-lane, perfectly paved road, but with a huge speed bump[1] off in the distance labelled "political reform: how in the world do we get from
5 Communism to a more open society?" When 1.3 billion people going 130 kilometers an hour hit a speed bump one of two things happens: Either the car flies into the air and slams down, and all the parts hold together and it keeps on moving – or the car flies into the air, slams down and all the wheels fall off. Which it will be with China, I don't know. India, by contrast, is like a highway full of potholes[2], with no sidewalks
10 and half the streetlamps broken. But off in the distance, the road seems to smooth out, and if it does, this country will be a dynamo. The question is: Is that smoother road in the distance a mirage or the real thing? [...]
"The ecosystem for innovation is now starting to be created here," said Nandan Nilekani, the chief executive officer of Infosys. For several years now, when venture[3] capi-
15 talists funded companies in the United States, they insisted that the research and development for the products be done in India. But now, increasingly, Western companies will come up with a new idea and then tell Infosys, Wipro or Tata, India's premier technology companies, to research, develop and produce the whole thing.
As one Wipro executive put it, "You go from solving my problem to serving my busi-
20 ness to knowing my business to being my business." What will be left for the Western companies is the "ideation," the original concept and design of a flagship product[4] (which is a major undertaking), and then the sales and marketing.
"We're going from a model of doing piecework to where the entire product and entire innovation stream is done by companies here," Mr. Nikelani added. All of this means
25 that innovation will happen faster and cheaper, with much more global collaboration. The best indication that Bangalore is becoming hot is how many foreign technology professionals – non-Indians – are now coming here to work. P. Anandan, an Indian-American who worked for Microsoft or for 28 years in Redmond, Washington, just opened Microsoft's research center in Bangalore, which follows the ones in Redmond,
30 Cambridge and Beijng. "I have two non-Indians working for me here, one Japanese and one American, and they could work anywhere in the world," Mr. Anandan said. He added that when he got his engineering degree in India 28 years ago, all the competition was to get a job abroad. Now the fiercest competition is to get an I.T. job in India: "It is no longer, 'Well I have to stay here,' but, 'Do I get a chance to stay
35 here?'"
In the past year, Infosys received 9,600 applications from abroad, including from China, France and Germany, for internships, and it accepted 100. I asked one of these interns, Vicky Chen, a Chinese-American business student from the Claremont Col-

---

[1]**speed bump** obstacle in a street to make cars slow down   [2]**pothole** hole in the surface of a road   [3]**venture capital** money invested in a new enterprise, esp. a risky one   [4]**flagship product** most important of a group of products

Klausur

leges, why she came. "All the business is coming to India, and I don't see why I shouldn't follow the business," She said. "If this is where the center of gravity is, you should go check it out, and then you become more valuable." [40]

[...]

570 Wörter

Thomas L. Friedman, "Bangalore: Hot and Hotter", in: *The New York Times*, June 8, 2005

Activities

1. Illustrate the way production processes in India have changed over the years.

2. Describe the job situation in Indian high-tech companies.

3. Analyse the use of metaphors in the text.

4. Comment on the economic situation in present-day Indian society.

Klausur Solution

1. Illustrate the way production processes in India have changed over the years.

Production processes in India have undergone major changes over the past few years. Some years ago Western companies outsourced the research and development for new products to Indian companies, which meant only small parts of the whole production process were done in India, but the decisive and important decisions and actions rested with Western industry. Nowadays this is different. Western companies increasingly leave the complete production process with their Indian business partners and only contribute the ideas for a new product and take care of its marketing. Everything else, from research to development to the complete production, is done by Indian companies like Infosys, Wipro or Tata.

2. Describe the job situation in Indian high-tech companies.

The dream of Indian IT engineers used to be to get a good education in India and then leave the country to work somewhere in the West. This is no longer the case. As more and more Western companies such as Microsoft, for example, open up businesses in India and as more and more Indian IT companies become global players not only do Indian engineers dream of being offered a job at home, but engineers and management experts from abroad come to India for a career. As one Chinese-American business student put it, "All the business is coming to India."

3. Analyze the metaphorical language of the text.

The author of the text uses one extensive metaphor. He compares India and China to roads and the Indian and Chinese economies to cars driving on these roads.

The Chinese road is a six-lane, perfectly paved road, which means theoretically China offers its economy a perfect infrastructure, but there is a huge speed-bump in the distance, which represents the political obstacles a future Chinese economy has to overcome before it can play its part in the global market, i. e. its strictly regulated present economy which is dominated by communist ideas of five-year plans. The question is whether the Chinese economy can survive a clash with its own communist ideas and continue on a road of reforms or whether it will finally be destroyed by these ideas.

The Indian road, on the other hand, is far from perfect, full of potholes with broken street lamps, and so it is very difficult to drive on. However, there seems to be a better road ahead, which will enable the engine of the Indian industry to run on smoothly and the question here is, whether this better road in the distance is real or only a vision. Friedman's text indicates that the former is the case.

4. Comment on the economic situation in present-day Indian society.

Present-day Indian society seems to be divided into two parts. There is rural India with its predominantly medieval production processes, and there is urban India, or at least a small part of urban India, with its booming IT industry.

In rural India, many people live like their ancestors hundreds of years ago, without the aid of machines or modern technology. Children only get very basic schooling and hardly any further education. Girls and women are still less than second-class citizens with no rights at all. Rural society is very much dominated by the idea of caste which prohibits development and modernization.

Klausur Solution

While rural India seems in many respects still deeply rooted in the past, parts of urban India have made their way well into the 21st century. Middle-class children – boys and girls – get the best education their parents can afford and after attending India's elite universities and colleges they are offered jobs by the booming IT industry with incomes their fellow-countrymen from poorer parts of India can only dream of.

This reality is far from what Mahatma Gandhi envisaged when he fought for Indian independence. India will have to work towards a more equal society with chances for everybody, no matter where they are from and what caste they belong to, if it wants to ensure a stable society and a prosperous future for all its citizens.

Bollywood Dreams

Jonathan Torgovnik

Author and text

Jonathan Torgovnik has been a well-known photographer for *Newsweek Magazine* since 2005 and is on the Faculty of the International Center of Photography School in New York. He graduated with a BFA degree from the School of Visual Arts in New York. His photographs from various projects and assignments have been published in numerous international publications including *Newsweek*, *GEO*, *The Sunday Times Magazine* and others. Torgovnik is the author of *Bollywood Dreams*, an exploration of the motion picture industry and its culture in India.

The first part of his expository text highlights the characteristics of Bollywood films (songs, dances, contents); and in the second part, the history of Indian cinema is retraced.

Unterrichtsempfehlungen

Als Einstieg ist ein Akrostichon denkbar, das die Lehrkraft an die Tafel schreibt. Die Schülerinnen und Schüler kommen nach vorn und schreiben die Assoziationen, die sie mit dem Begriff Hollywood verbinden, auf. Vorher wird geklärt, ob jeweils der erste Buchstabe als Wortanfang genommen werden muss oder ob als Erleichterung auch Buchstaben darum herum gruppiert werden dürfen.

```
              P H OTOGRAPH
          ACT O R
           FI L MS
           CA L IFORNIA
   FILMINDUSTR Y
          MAE W EST
            M O NEY
            L O CATION
           VI D EO
```

Falls die Schülerinnen und Schüler bereits mit dem Begriff Hollywood vertraut sind, kann ein analoges Akrostichon zu Bollywood erstellt werden.

Aufgaben 6 und 7 können, je nach Ausführlichkeit der Bearbeitung, als gleichwertige Feststellung von Schülerleistungen herangezogen werden.

Eine Auflistung bekannter Bollywoodfilme kann in Aufgabe 7 wie folgt aussehen:
1) Kuch Kuch Hota Hai
2) Dil Se
3) Satyra
4) Dilwale Dulhany Le Jaynge
5) 1942: A Love Story
6) Dil Chahta Hai
7) Zakhm
8) Lagaan
9) Satta

10) Qayamat Se Qayamat Tak
11) Swades - We, the people
12) Ver-Zaara
und viele andere mehr

Solutions

Activities p. 40

1. Describe the typical make-up of Bollywood films.

Bollywood films very much resemble storytelling, yet they always have special ingredients such as song and dance numbers. Bollywood films mostly talk about absolute love, about conflicts within the family, mostly between fathers and sons as well as about revenge, redemption, self-respect and religious and moral values. Moreover, typical of Bollywood films are cinematic devices: repetition is a key concept as well as the starring of well-known actors. Furthermore the right kind of music and extraordinary sets and places are a must if the film is to be successful. What the Indian audience wants are loud action scenes as well as a happy ending. Usual Bollywood films are two and a half to three hours long.

2. Identify the elements of Indian culture contained in Bollywood films.

Bollywood films use a mixture of two of the traditional languages spoken in India: Hindi and Urdu. Elements of Indian culture such as class, religion and tradition are incorporated in the films. Very often Bollywood films borrow plots from Hollywood films, but they are reworked according to the rules of Bollywood make-up, so that in the end the origin of the plot can hardly be recognized.

3. Retrace the history of Indian cinema.

At the beginning, Indian films were silent. They were inspired by well-known Hindu epic tales in which gods fought with demons. The mythological contents could be manifested to maximum effect by using newly invented camera techniques such as special effects or low-angle shots. Other features of Indian culture such as the theatrical forms, Ram Leela and Ras Leela, made their way into Indian cinema: representations of exploits carried out by the gods, Ram and Krishna, are still today reflected in the working together of music and drama and in the representation of important characters.

Early Indian film productions took place in tents next to temples in villages and small towns. In the late 1940s the studio era ended and film production was shifted to big cities.

4. Outline how Bollywood films are produced today.

Today we are witnessing a real mass production of Bollywood films. Everybody involved in the production of a Bollywood film – from the most influential director to the least important technician – works on several films at the same time. Stars travel from one set to another, playing completely different roles in each film. This simultaneousness in production is due to economic and financial constraints. Since nobody can guarantee the success of a certain film, an alternative is always in the pipeline.

5. Sum up the importance of Indian cinema to the Indians.

Indian cinema is extremely important to the Indians. Their daily routine is marked by the films. There are huge signs and ads influenced by Bollywood in almost every city. Indians feel attracted by and connected to the films because they admire a particular aspect: a star, a song or a dance. Indians living abroad consider Bollywood films as a link to their home country.

6. **Familiarize yourself with Sahshi Tharoor, *Show Business*, New York 1992, Arcade Publishing. Work out to what extent the book reflects the information in the given text.**

   Show Business begins with Ashok Banjara, a superstar in Bollywood, fighting for his life in the intensive care unit of a hospital after an accident on the set of a film that he is shooting. Suspended between life and death he sees his entire life in Bollywood flashing in front of his eyes like a film. Details of Banjara's career in Bollywood are revealed primarily in flashback.

   A young Ashok Banjara leaves Delhi and comes to Bombay to make his fortune and find fame in Bollywood. He achieves the big league with his second film *Godambo* that establishes him as an action star. Soon Banjara is known for playing the role of an angry young man fighting for the poor and the helpless against the establishment. A successful Ashok Banjara marries Maya, a talented co-star, and convinces her to stay away from films for the sake of family. Banjara, though, is something of a philanderer, going to bed with most of his heroines. The actress Mehnaz Elahi becomes his mistress.

   At the pinnacle of his success as a Bollywood star, Banjara is enticed to join politics and wins the election easily (in his politician father's constituency). However, to his dismay, he finds that the party has no significant role for him and he languishes in the back benches in parliament. Meanwhile Banjara makes a film, *Mechanic*, which is his first flop.

   Sometime later Banjara is implicated in a money-laundering scandal. His party extricates him by saying that he is irrelevant in the party's scheme of things. Banjara quits politics. The scandal has destroyed his fortune and Banjara finds that he has to seek work again. With no mainstream director or producer ready to cast him now, he agrees to work in a mythological film in desperation (he hates mythologicals) called *Kalki*. It is on the sets of *Kalki* that Banjara meets his accident. Fate is not without its sense of irony. *Kalki* is supposed to be Banjara's comeback vehicle – one that will restore his fortunes and once again establish him solidly with his audience. Banjara's accident on the set of *Kalki* sees an audience of hundreds gathered outside the hospital waiting for news of his health. Millions of others are praying for his recovery from their homes.

   Show Business is the literary transposition of an actual everyday practice in the Indian film production industry.

7. **Choose one of the numerous Bollywood films available at present on TV or DVD and present it in class. For the presentation take into consideration the plot, the actors, the male and female protagonists, the stage props and the message of the film. Individual answers are expected.**

   Hilfe im Dschungel der zahlosen Bollywoodproduktionen bietet u. a. Christian Lukas, Bollywood. Die besten Filme und ihre Stars, Heel Verlag, Königswinter 2006.

The Great King Khan

Malcolm Beith

Malcolm Beith is a general editor at *Newsweek International*. He lives in New York City. The interview gives insight into various aspects of Shahrukh Khan, his attitude towards Buddhism, the importance he ascribes to songs in Bollywood films, the power of escapism and the future of Bollywood films.

Author and text

Unterrichtsempfehlungen

In einem Assoziogramm werden Informationen zu Shahrukh Khan an der Tafel gesammelt, die von den Schülerinnen und Schülern ins Heft übernommen werden. Sie können später als Baustein für Aufgabe 4 verwendet werden.

Aufgabe 4 kann als Hot seat durchgeführt werden. Ein(e) Schüler(in), die sich selbst als SRK-Experten/in ansieht, nimmt auf dem Hot seat Platz und beantwortet die Fragen, die die Mitschüler stellen. Sie/Er kann sich noch einen Berater wählen.
Mögliche Fragen, die an Shahrukh Khan gestellt werden können:
1) If you weren't successful as an actor, what would you do?
I could work as an author or as an advisor.

2) Why haven't you turned to Buddhism yet?
Although I consider Buddhism a highly positive religion, I am a firm believer of Islam.

Solutions

Activities p. 42

1. Comment on Khan's nickname.
Khan's nickname is "King Khan". (King Kong is an association that also comes to mind.) Taking into consideration his fame and success, it becomes clear that it is a well-chosen nickname for him. The artist doesn't only star in many films, he is also a famous film producer himself, and so a leading figure in different areas of the film industry. It is very easy to understand why he acquired the attribute "king".

2. Explain what Buddhism means to Khan.
Khan himself is a Muslim and his wife is a Hindu. Yet Buddhism is the religion that provides the path to peace according to Khan. For Khan Buddhism has the advantage of being neutral, a religion that does not display features of fanaticism or fundamentalism. Compared to Islam or Christianity, Khan thinks that Buddhism is more moderate and universal. Through Buddhism, so Khan, everyone can understand that they speak the same universal human language.

3. Explain the importance of escapism.
In the films, the audience wants to be entertained, and to get away from the problems and monotony of everyday life. People want to take refuge in fantastic worlds, and the songs and dances in Hindi films enhance their escapist nature.

4. Get more information about Khan.
Wikipedia can be used as a starting point: http://www.wikipedia.org

5. Globalization is the overriding principle in present-day society. Discuss its impact on the arts.
As well as in every other domain in modern life, globalization has made its way to the arts, too. Let's take the field of music for example. Young people all over the world just couldn't do without music from other cultures. Everybody from all over the world listens to music from Africa, America, Asia, Australia and Europe. You can turn on the radio in good old Germany and come across songs people in India like to listen to. The same is true for films; you don't have to be in Africa in order to be able to watch an African film in the cinema or on TV. Also special ways of dancing, e.g. the Bollywood dances, are performed by people all over the world.

Worksheet 5

Hollywood vs Bollywood vs Kollywood

It is a well-known fact that the Indian movie industry is extremely productive. Next to Bollywood there are more movements, one of them being Kollywood (others are Tollywood, Lollywood etc.) Find out about its particularities and contrast them to Hollywood and Bollywood.

	Hollywood	Bollywood	Kollywood
What is meant in this context by			
Language used in films			
Place of film production			
Number of films produced in a) 1975 b) 1985 c) 1995	a) b) c)	a) b) c)	a) b) c)
Main topics			
Make-up of the films			
Name three famous films	– – –	– – –	– – –
Name three famous actors	– – –	– – –	– – –

Worksheet 5 Solution

Hollywood vs Bollywood vs Kollywood

Die von den Schülern genannten Namen von Schauspielern und Filmen werden individuell unterschiedlich sein.

	Hollywood	Bollywood	Kollywood
What is meant in this context by	American films, mainly produced to entertain and for commercial reasons	Indian films produced to entertain an Indian audience	Indian films produced to entertain an Indian audience, Bollywood is taken as an example
Language used in films	English	Hindi or Urdu	Tamil
Place of film production	Hollywood	Mumbay (formerly Bombay)	Chennai (formerly Madras)
Number of films produced in a) 1975 b) 1985 c) 1995	a) 258 b) 356 c) 631	a) 119 b) 185 c) 157	a) 70 b) 190 c) 165
Main topics	Love stories	Love stories, Indian culture and traditions	Love stories, Indian culture and traditions
Make-up of the films	Expensive films Many special effects	Songs, dances Exotic locations, colourful settings	Songs, dances Exotic locations, colourful settings
Name three famous films		– Indian Love Story – Veer and Zaara – Swades	– Chandramukhi – Anniyan – Sivayi
Name three famous actors		– SRK – Rani Mukherji – Amitabh Bachchan	– Sivaji Ganesan – Tamil Nadus – Rajinikanth

In Search of an Identity

Passage to India

E. M. Forster

Author and text

Edward Morgan Forster (1879–1970) was an English writer who is famous for his ironic novels examining class difference in early 20th century British society. He studied at King's College, Cambridge between 1897 and 1901. After leaving university he went on a journey which took him to India, among other countries. In the early 1920s he again spent some time in India as the private secretary to the Maharajah of Devas. Following his return from India in 1924, he published his last novel, *A Passage to India*.

The main characters in *A Passage to India* are the Englishman, Cyril Fielding, his Indian friend, Dr Aziz, and Adela Quested, a British school teacher who has come to India with her future mother-in-law, Mrs Moore, to get married to Mrs Moore's son, Ronny Heaslop, who is a city magistrate in the city of Chandrapore. After a trip to the Marabar Caves Adela accuses Aziz of having sexually assaulted her. During Aziz's trial the racial tensions and prejudices between Indians and the British colonists become obvious. Only Cyril Fielding stands by his Indian friend and is condemned by his fellow countrymen as a traitor. At the trial Adela Quested withdraws her accusations and the case is dismissed. Aziz is angry with Fielding for having let Adela stay in his house until her departure for Britain and vows never to be friends with a British person again. Fielding leaves for Britain, too. Two years later the two men meet and become friends again, but they both know that the time is not yet for the Indians and the British to be friends and that India is not the place where such a friendship could prosper.

The two excerpts are taken from the second and from the last chapters of Forster's novel, when Aziz and Mrs Moore meet for the first time, and when Fielding and Aziz say their last goodbyes.

Unterrichtsempfehlungen

Als Vorbereitung für die Beschäftigung mit dem Auszug aus Forsters Roman können die Schülerinnen und Schüler aufgefordert werden, sich in einem englischen Literaturlexikon oder im Internet (z. B. http://www.bookrags.com/notes/pti) mit dem Inhalt von *A Passage to India* und der dort thematisierten Problematik des Verhältnisses von britischen Kolonialherren und Indern vertraut zu machen.

Eine Annäherung an das im Textauszug beschriebene Aufeinandertreffen zweier Vertreter verschiedener religiöser Glaubensgemeinschaften kann über ein kurzes Unterrichtsgespräch über ähnliche Erfahrungen auf Urlaubsreisen geleistet werden. Folgende Impulsfragen können hier eingesetzt werden:

- Have you had similar experiences on holidays, for example, when you found it was forbidden to enter a church in shorts, or when women were asked to cover their bare shoulders?
- How did you react in these situations? Did you follow the rules and visit the church, or did you think it was not worth the trouble?
- Do you think foreign tourists should be made to follow such rules, or are they only for the local population?

Zur Lösung von Aufgabe 4 arbeiten die Schülerinnen und Schüler in Kleingruppen. Sie erhalten den Auftrag, die wörtliche Rede aus dem Text zu isolieren und eine szenische Darstellung zu diskutieren. Je zwei Mitglieder jeder Gruppe führen ihre Interpretation des Gesprächs zwischen Aziz und Mrs Moore im Plenum auf. Die verschiedenen Ansätze werden im Anschluss an die Aufführungen diskutiert, wobei besonderer Wert auf Aziz' emotionale Verfassung gelegt werden sollte. Danach wird zur Frage übergeleitet, wie sich Aziz' Gefühle der ungerechten Behandlung durch die britischen Kolonialherren und deren Familien in seiner Sprache ausdrückt. Gegebenenfalls sollten mit den Schülerinnen und Schülern die in diesem Zusammenhang relevanten rhetorischen Figuren in einem kurzen Unterrichtsgespräch geklärt werden. Im Anschluss daran werden die Schülerinnen und Schüler aufgefordert, sich noch einmal mit dem Text zu beschäftigen, Beispiele zu finden und diese zu kategorisieren. Dies kann in den bereits zu Beginn eingeteilten Gruppen geschehen. Die Ergebnisse der abschließenden Gruppenarbeitsphase werden in die Kopiervorlage (Worksheet 6) eingetragen.

Die in Aufgabe 6 geforderten Interpretationen erarbeiten die Schülerinnen und Schüler in Einzelarbeit und stellen sie im Plenum vor.

In einer anschließenden Diskussion wird vor dem Hintergrund der Schülerarbeiten der Hauptaspekt des Vierzeilers „the secret understanding of the heart" (Z. 6 f.) thematisiert. Nun werden die Schülerinnen und Schüler aufgefordert, Textstellen zu finden, die diese von Aziz bewunderte menschliche Eigenschaft belegen und illustrieren. Die Ergebnisse werden an der Tafel gesammelt.

"The secret understanding of the heart!" (ll. 6 f.)

Mrs Moore	Aziz
– has taken off her shoes (ll. 16 ff.)	– blames Mrs Moore for not having taken off her shoes (ll. 14 f.)
– God is present in the mosque (ll. 25–38)	– God is present in the mosque (ll. 25–38)
– does not find Mrs Callendar charming (ll. 63 ff.)	– does not like Mrs Callendar because she is inconsiderate (ll. 63 ff.)
	↓
"I don't think I understand people very well. I only know whether I like them or dislike them." (ll. 85 ff.)	"Then you are an Oriental." (l. 87)

An dieser Stelle kann der Zusatztext vom Ende des Romans (Worksheet 7) eingesetzt werden.

Die im vorliegenden Textauszug wiedergegebene Begegnung der beiden aus unterschiedlichen Kulturen stammenden Figuren Aziz und Mrs Moore zeigt, wie im Gespräch gemeinsame Haltungen festgestellt und unterschiedliche Ansichten erläutert werden. Vor diesem Hintergrund sollen die Schülerinnen und Schüler die Probleme und die Möglichkeiten eines Austauschs zwischen den in Deutschland zusammen lebenden Kulturen diskutieren (Aufgabe 7). Zu diesem Zweck wird die Klasse in Gruppen eingeteilt, die den Auftrag erhalten, die Ergebnisse ihrer Diskussionen schriftlich festzuhalten. Nach der Gruppenarbeitsphase werden die Ergebnisse in eine vorbereitete Tabelle an der Tafel oder auf einer Overheadfolie eingetragen.

Der so erarbeitete Themenspeicher dient als Grundlage eines frei gehaltenen Kurzvortrags zum Thema „personal encounters as the basis for a multi-cultural society in Germany".

The problems and chances of personal encounters

problems

- closed communities prevent the need to talk, to open up or to meet
- no common language
- no places, reasons or chances to meet

chances

- getting to know other cultures, traditions and ways of thinking
- understanding unknown ways of behaviour
- looking at things from different points of view

Solutions

Activities p. 45

1. **Why is Aziz so angry at finding a European at the mosque?**
   Europeans usually do not respect the code of behaviour in a mosque. Aziz assumes that the strange woman, being European, has not taken off her shoes and that this has violated his holy place of prayer.

2. **How does Mrs Moore change Aziz's initial indignation?**
   Aziz is surprised when he finds that Mrs Moore has actually taken off her shoes, which means she shows respect for the rules of another religion and for Aziz's feelings as a pious man. To Aziz, finding such behaviour in a European is very unusual. Moreover, Aziz learns that Mrs Moore feels the same way about God's presence in holy places as he does. To her it does not seem to make any difference that she is a Christian in a Muslim place of worship. God is wherever there are people seeking him.

3. **What does this excerpt tell the reader about the relationship between the British and the Indians in British India?**
   Aziz's surprise at Mrs Moore's respectful behaviour towards himself and his creed indicates that such behaviour is unusual in Europeans.
   There is further evidence for this attitude when Aziz tells Mrs Moore about the way he is treated by British officials like the civil surgeon and his wife. They show no consideration for the feelings of Indians. The civil surgeon calls Aziz in his free time for no reason at all forcing Aziz to leave his friends and making him wait outside his house without being at home. On this particular night the civil surgeon's wife even took Aziz's carriage without asking him, making Aziz walk all the way back. Aziz's description of his relationship to the British culminates in the fact that Indians are not allowed in the Chandrapore Club even as guests.

4. **Concentrate on the second part of the excerpt (ll. 58 ff.) and explain how the narrator conveys Aziz's agitation by the way he talks.**

Aziz's language

sentence structure	examples	Aziz's state of mind
complete sentences, correct grammar	Would you care to see over the Minto Hospital one morning? (l. 58) I have nothing else to offer at Chandrapore. (l. 59) I suppose the civil surgeon took you. (l. 62)	calmness
exclamations	Ah! (l. 64) ..., yes, yes, ... (l. 75) Oh, if others resembled you! (l. 84)	agitation
one-word questions	What? What? (l. 66)	

sentence structure	examples	Aziz's state of mind
repetitions	What? What? (l. 66) ... – do you call that being charming? (ll. 69 f.) ... Is this charming, pray? (ll. 72 f.) You understand me, you know what I feel. (l. 84)	
rhetorical questions	You didn't like her? (l. 66) ... – do you call that being charming? (ll. 69 f.) Is this charming, pray? (ll. 72 f.) But what does it matter? (l. 73)	
elliptic sentences	A very charming lady. (l. 64) ... and not even a message. (l. 72) ..., if others resembled you! (l. 84)	
polysyndetons	– and Major Callendar interrupts me night after night from where I am dining with my friends and I go at once, ..., and he is not there and not even a message. (ll. 70 ff.) ... and Mrs Callendar takes my carriage and cuts me dead ... (ll. 75 ff.)	
complete sentences, correct grammar	Then you are an Oriental. (l. 87) Indians are not allowed into the Chandrapore Club even as guests. (l. 90)	calmness, resignation

5. **Describe Aziz's self-confidence as an Indian as it is alluded to in the text.**

Aziz's self-confidence as an Indian can be seen at the beginning and towards the end of the excerpt. It is hinted at when he addresses Mrs Moore rather angrily and tells her that she is not welcome in the mosque, reproaching her for not having taken off her shoes.

Azizs's self-confidence as an Indian becomes more obvious in the course of his conversation with Mrs Moore, especially when he talks about the behaviour of the British in general, and his personal experiences with them in particular.

The British hurt Indians by their neglect of Indian traditions, customs and values and by their lack of respect. Not only do they desecrate Muslim places of worship by their disregard of the rules of Islam, they also treat Indians like servants, no matter what their social position is or what education they have. Aziz feels that this treatment is wrong and when he finds that Mrs Moore is sympathetic to him rather than to her fellow-countrymen, he can't help complaining about the way he is treated by people like the civil surgeon and his wife.

They use him like a servant, without taking into consideration his own plans and wishes. In the course of his speech, Aziz assumes the point of view of a British person and when he asks "But what does it matter?" (l. 73) and adds "I am just as a subordinate, my time is of no value, and Mrs Callendar takes my carriage and cuts me dead ..." (ll. 74 ff.) he wants to express the opposite. It does matter to him that he is bossed around and he is angry about being a subordinate and that the veranda is not good enough for him. His time is of value to him.

Unlike the British, an oriental does not judge people by what they are or where they are from. He likes or dislikes them for what they are like and this is enough (ll. 85 ff.). Aziz's final remarks about Indians not being allowed into the Chandrapore Club, however, show that his fury about the injustice of British rule does not go beyond words. In the end he accepts them as facts that cannot be altered.

6. **Write down a one-sentence interpretation of the quatrain at the beginning of the excerpt. To what extent can it be seen as a motto for the following action?**

   "Time will go on beyond my own death, but I will not be forgotten as long as there are people who feel as I felt."

   This sentence can be seen as the motto of the following action because Mrs Moore and Aziz feel the same about religion, certain members of the British society of Chandrapore and the relationship between the British and Indians.

   On a larger scale it also describes the relationship between Aziz and Fielding throughout the novel as is exemplified in the excerpt from the last chapter (Worksheet 7).

7. **Getting to know each other helps to break down prejudices. What are the problems and what are the chances for success of this attitude in our society?**

   Ladies and Gentlemen,

   In the following I am going to give a short talk on whether personal encounters can be the basis for a multi-cultural society in Germany.

   Let me begin with the problems and then move on to the chances. Migrants often live in closed communities, which means they live in the same parts of a town, where they have their own shops, places of worship, restaurants or cafés and other places where they can meet and talk in their own languages. They leave these voluntary ghettos only to go to work or to school. This situation gives them security and the illusion of still being in their native countries. So they do not feel the necessity to meet Germans or members of other minority groups in German society.

   There are not many places or events where migrants and Germans can meet because the majority of Germans do not feel the need to get to know and talk to members of minorities.

   Once meetings between cultures do take place these can open up priceless chances for the realization of a multi-cultural society. Getting to know other cultures, traditions and ways of thinking makes it easier to understand other people's behaviour. It also helps to look at things from a point of view different to one's own, as this is an enriching experience in itself which again helps to understand other people.

   In conclusion, I think it is very important that people from different ethnic groups in Germany should meet and get to know each other because this will change their individual lives and our society as a whole.

Worksheet 6

Aziz's Language

Work in small groups and fill in the grid.

sentence structure	examples	Aziz's state of mind
complete sentences, correct grammar		
exclamations		
one-word questions		
repetitions		
rhetorical questions		
elliptic sentences		
polysyndetons		
complete sentences, correct grammar		

Worksheet 7

A Passage to India

E. M. Forster

"Oh, shut up," he said. "Don't spoil our last hour with foolish questions. Leave Krishna[1] alone, and talk about something sensible."

They did. All the way back to Mau[2] they wrangled[3] about politics. Each had hardened since Chandrapore, and a good knock-about[4] proved enjoyable. They trusted each
5 other, although they were going to part, perhaps because they were going to part. Fielding had "no further use for politeness," he said, meaning that the British Empire really can't be abolished because it's rude. Aziz retorted, "Very well, and we have no use for you," and glared at him with abstract hate.

[...] Aziz grew more excited. He rose in his stirrups[5] and pulled at his horse's head in
10 the hope it would rear[6]. Then he should feel in battle. He cried: "Clear out, all you Turtons and Burtons[7]. We wanted to know you ten years back – now it's too late. If we see you and sit on your committees, it's for political reasons, don't you make any mistake." His horse did rear. "Clear out, clear out, I say. Why are we put to so much suffering? We used to blame you, now we blame ourselves, we grow wiser. Until England
15 is in difficulties we keep silent, but in the next European war aha, aha! Then is our time." [...] Fielding mocked again. And Aziz in an awful rage danced this way and that, not knowing what to do, and cried: "Down with the English anyhow. That's certain. Clear out, you fellows, double quick, I say. We may hate one another, but we hate you most. If I don't make you go, Ahmed will, Karim[8] will, if it's fifty or five hundred years
20 we shall get rid of you, yes, yes, we shall drive every blasted Englishman into the sea, and then" – he rode against him furiously – "and then," he concluded, half kissing him, "you and I shall be friends." "Why can't we be friends now?" said the other, holding him affectionately. "It's what I want. It's what you want."

But the horses didn't want it – they swerved[9] apart; the earth didn't want it, sending
25 up rocks through which riders must pass single-file[10]; the temples, the tank, the jail, the palace, the birds, the carrion[11], the Guest House, that came into view as they issued from the gap and saw Mau beneath: they didn't want it, they said in their hundred voices, "No, not yet," and the sky said, "No, not there."

E. M. Forster, A Passage to India, Penguin Books, London 1989 , pp. 314–316; © The Provost and Scholars of King's College, Cambridge, and The Society of Authors as the Literary Representatives of the Estate of E. M. Forster

---

[1]**Krishna** most celebrated Hindu deity   [2]**Mau** Indian town in the novel   [3]**to wrangle** to argue   [4]**knock-about** silly, entertaining argument   [5]**stirrup** *Steigbügel*   [6]**to rear** (of a horse) to raise itself on its hind legs   [7]**Turtons and Burtons** surnames sounding typically British and therefore representing the British in general   [8]**Ahmed and Karim** Aziz's sons   [9]**to swerve** to change direction suddenly   [10]**single-file** moving one after another   [11]**carrion** dead and decaying flesh

Activities

1. **Describe Aziz's attitude towards the relationship between the Indians and the British and compare it to his ideas from the excerpt in the pupils' book.**

2. **How does the narrator judge the chances of Indians and Europeans ever becoming friends?**

Worksheet 7 Solutions

1. Describe Aziz's attitude towards the relationship between the Indians and the British and compare it to his ideas from the excerpt in the pupils' book.

In the last chapter of Forster's novel Aziz distinguishes between personal relationships and the relationship between the Indians and the British. Although the former is possible – he has still got a British friend – he is convinced that there cannot be a friendly relationship between India and Britain.

While at the beginning of the novel Aziz longed to be accepted by the British as an equal and is deeply offended by the way he is treated by them, at the end of the novel he is proud and self-confident enough to believe in India's power to free itself from the British. The sufferings and injustices imposed upon the Indians by the British have enabled the Indian people to overcome the hostilities that divided them, and to form one Indian nation strong enough to fight the British and finally expel them from the country. Aziz is certain that Indian independence from Britain will become reality one day.

2. How does the narrator judge the chances of Indians and Europeans ever becoming friends?

In the characters of Aziz and Fielding, the narrator hints at the possibility of friendship between the Indians and the British, but he also makes it clear that this friendship cannot last because in the last chapter of the novel Aziz and Fielding meet for the last time and it is clear to them both that they will not see each other again. This is because the time has not yet come when Indians and Europeans can be equals, and India is not a place where they can meet as equal partners.

In negating this possibility for the time and place of the novel, however, the narrator opens up the possibility of friendship and partnership between the Indians and the British or Indians and Europeans for the future.

Benaras Hindu University Speech

Mahatma Gandhi

Mohandas Karamchand Gandhi was born in Probandar, Gujarat, on 2nd October, 1869. **Author and text**
He was born into *vaishya*, the business caste. In May 1882 he was married to Kasturba
Makharij. They had four sons. In 1888 Gandhi went to University College, London, to
train as a barrister and was finally admitted to the Bar in Britain. After unsuccessfully
trying to establish himself as a lawyer in India, he went to Natal, South Africa, where he
worked for an Indian firm. Here he encountered and experienced racism on various
occasions, which made him question his people's status and his own place in society.
The situation of Indians in South Africa deteriorated and at a protest meeting in Johan-
nesburg Ghandhi pronounced his ideal of *satyagraha*, non-violent resistance, for the
first time.
In 1915 he returned to India and began to transform his habits and lifestyle to more
traditional Indian ways. At this time he also began his work for Indian independence.
After the Amritsar Massacre in Punjab, where almost 400 civilians were killed by British
troops, Gandhi condemned violence on both sides, saying that all violence was evil and
could not be justified. At this time he started to focus on obtaining complete self-gov-
ernment for India, aiming at complete individual, spiritual and political independence.
In April 1920 Gandhi was elected president of the All India Home Rule League and one
year later was given executive authority on behalf of the Indian National Congress
whose aim was Indian independence. In March 1930 he launched a campaign against
the tax on salt, emphasizing his demands by the famous Salt March to Dandi (21
March – 6 April, 1930).
During the Second World War he gave a series of speeches, the "Quit India Speeches",
where he called on the British to leave India. At the end of the Second World War the
British were ready to transfer all power to India.
After the war Gandhi was against the separation of Muslim-dominated Pakistan from
Hindu-dominated India. He devoted the last years of his life to the reconciliation of the
two parties.
On 30 January, 1948 Gandhi was shot dead on his way to a prayer meeting by a radical
Hindu who was critical of his policy of reconciliation.
The text is an excerpt from a speech made by Gandhi at the opening of the Benaras
Hindu University on 4 February, 1916. Gandhi talks about the power of vernacular lan-
guages in the nation-building process and deals with the issue of anarchy and the ne-
cessity of violence to realize political ideas.

Unterrichtsempfehlungen

Die die Beschäftigung mit dem Text einleitende Recherche zum Leben und Wirken
Gandhis sollte in Gruppenarbeit organisiert werden. Folgende Internetseite bietet umfassende Informationen zu diesem Thema: http://www.mkgandhi.org
Zur Lösung von Aufgabe 3 kann auf die im Rahmen der Beschäftigung mit dem Textauszug von E. M. Forster (S. 45, Aufg. 4) erarbeiteten rhetorischen Figuren zurückge-
griffen werden. Die Schülerinnen und Schüler erhalten zunächst den Auftrag, den Text
im Hinblick auf rhetorische Figuren zu lesen und relevante Passagen zu unterstrei-
chen. Nachdem geklärt ist, von welchen Figuren Gandhi Gebrauch macht, werden die
entsprechenden Beispiele an der Tafel gesammelt. Um den Tafelanschrieb auf einen
sinnvollen Umfang zu reduzieren, können für die Rubriken „rhetorical questions" und
„asyndeta" zwei bis drei Beispiele ausgewählt werden.

Gandhi's style

elliptical sentences
In Bombay, mind you, not in Benaras ... (ll. 4 f.)
Why this handicap to the nation? (l. 11)

exclamations
In Bombay, mind you, ... (l. 4)

rhetorical questions
... will you believe me when I tell you that the only speeches that touched the huge audience in Bombay were the speeches that were delivered in Hindustani? (ll. 2 ff.)
Is there a man who dreams that English can ever become the national language of India? (ll. 10 f.)

asyndeta
We may foam, we may fret, we may resent, ... (l. 37)
... we shall have to fear no one, not the Maharajas, not the Viceroys, not the detectives, not even King George. (ll. 42 ff.)

addresses to the audience
... and if you tell me ..., then say ... (ll. 8 f.)
But let us not forget ... (l. 37 f.)

repetitions
..., what should we have today? – We should have today a free India, we should have our educated men, ... (ll. 26 ff.)
I honour the anarchist ... – I honour him ... (l. 45)

Gandhi uses rhetorical questions, asyndeta, and repetitions to convince his audience. He faces the audience and formulates exclamations and elliptical sentences to give the impression that he is talking directly to every single member

Um sicherzustellen, dass den Schülerinnen und Schülern die Grundlagen für das Formulieren von if-Sätzen präsent sind (Aufgabe 4), kann nach der Recherche die folgende Tabelle thematisiert werden.

if-clauses

type	if-clause	main clause	usage
I	present tense	will, can, may, etc. + infinitive	the actions expressed in the main clause are likely to happen
II	past tense	conditional I (would, could, might, etc. + infinitive)	the actions expressed in the main clause are theoretically possible but practically unlikely
III	past perfect	conditional II (would have, could have, might have, etc. + past participle)	the actions expressed in the main clause can no longer be fulfilled as the conditions expressed in the if-clause refer to the past

Da Aufgabe 5 für Schülerinnen und Schüler recht anspruchsvoll ist, sollen sie durch eine kurze Übung an die in der Aufgabenstellung thematisierte Problematik herangeführt werden. Die Schülerinnen und Schüler werden aufgefordert, ihr momentanes Befinden in zwei bis drei Sätzen schriftlich auf Englisch zu formulieren. Dann sollen sie dasselbe auf Deutsch bzw. in ihrer Muttersprache tun. In einer anschließenden Diskussion soll herausgefunden werden, welche Schwierigkeiten sich bei der Formulierung der eigenen Befindlichkeit in der Fremdsprache ergeben haben. Idealerweise wird aus dieser Übung deutlich werden, dass es bei der Formulierung in der Fremdsprache neben den sprachlichen Schwierigkeiten (Wortwahl, Grammatik) auch emotionale Barrieren zu überwinden gilt, die beim Sprechen der Muttersprache nicht existieren. Die Ergebnisse der Diskussion werden an der Tafel gesammelt und dienen als Grundlage für die schriftliche Ausarbeitung.

Our languages are the reflections of ourselves (ll. 7 f.)

- A person's feelings and personality are best expressed in their own language.
- Languages reflect the character of an individual, but also of a people and its country or region, e. g. rural areas have more words dealing with agriculture than urban areas.
- Language reflects the state of one's education, e. g. more educated people have got a bigger and a more elaborate vocabulary.
- A foreign language will never be as emotionally close to a speaker as their native language, e. g. native languages are used in emotional situations such as scolding or swearing.

Solutions

1. **Explain the special power of vernacular languages as described in the text and discuss the advantages of the use of vernacular languages in the nation building process.**

   Vernaculars have the power to touch people more intensely than foreign languages because they come from the heart and are much closer to people. So vernacular languages should also be the official languages of a country.

   If vernacular languages are used in all fields of life, such as science or politics, this saves people the trouble of first learning a foreign language and so saves them a lot of precious time. If education is based on the vernacular language of a nation this strengthens people's confidence and pride in their own county and their feeling of unity.

   Activity p. 47

2. **What does Gandhi say about violence as a means of anarchy?**

   Gandhi distinguishes between violent and non-violent anarchy. The former he says, has no room in India (l. 41), because it is a sign of fear. Gandhi can understand the motivation of those anarchists who use violence as a means to attain their aims, for he, too, loves his country, but according to him killing is not honourable and it is against the laws of God and man.

   Activities p. 48

3. **Comment on Gandhi's style. Identify the rhetorical devices he makes use of and find examples from the text.**

   elliptical sentences
   In Bombay, mind you, not in Benaras ... (ll. 4 f.)
   Why this handicap to the nation? (l. 11)

   exclamations
   In Bombay, mind you, ... (l. 4)

   rhetorical questions
   ... will you believe me when I tell you that the only speeches that touched the huge audience in Bombay were the speeches that were delivered in Hindustani? (ll. 2 ff.)
   Is there a man who dreams that English can ever become the national language of India? (ll. 10 f.)
   Why this handicap to the nation? (l. 11)

How can we have any … (ll. 19 ff.)
…, what should we have today? (l. 26 f.)
Is it not better that even Lord Hardinge should die …? (ll. 34 f.)
Is killing honourable? Is the dagger of an assassin a fit precursor for an honourable death? (ll. 47 f.)

<u>asyndeta</u>
We may foam, we may fret, we may resent, … (l. 37)
… we shall have to fear no one, not the Maharajas, not the Viceroys, not the detectives, not even King George. (ll. 42 ff.)

<u>addresses to the audience</u>
… and will you believe me when I tell you… (ll. 2 f.)
… mind you … (l. 4)
… and if you tell me …, then say … (ll. 8 f.)
Just consider for one moment … (l. 12)
Multiply that …, and find out … (ll. 17 f.)
But suppose … (l. 25)
But let us not forget … (l. 37 f.)

<u>repetitions</u>
what should we have today? – We should have today a free India, we should have our educated men, … (ll. 26 ff.)
I honour the anarchist … – I honour him … (l. 45)
… – is killing honourable? – … an honourable death? – … an honourable death. (ll. 47 ff.)

4. **Use your knowledge of English or use a grammar book to create an exercise about if-clauses for your partner. Your partner will do the same for you. Do the exercise and compare your results.**
   Exercises: if-clauses
   I. Name the type of if-clause and complete it.
   1) If you only worked a little harder, you would be really good at school. (II)
   2) If it goes on raining, I will stay at home. (I)
   3) If you had paid attention, I wouldn't have had to explain if-clauses again. (III)
   4) She'll never learn the truth if she doesn't ask him. (I)
   5) We couldn't manage this difficult situation if they didn't help us. (II)
   6) They could have had the time of their life on holiday if they hadn't quarrelled all the time. (III)

   II. Translate into English.
   1) Wenn du nicht so schnell gefahren wärst, hättest du keinen Strafzettel bekommen.
      If you hadn't driven so fast, you wouldn't have got a ticket.
   2) Ich wäre dir dankbar, wenn du etwas freundlicher zu ihnen wärst.
      I would be grateful if you were a little friendlier to them.
   3) Er wäre nicht gewählt worden, wenn er keine überzeugenden Argumente gehabt hätte.
      He wouldn't have been elected if he hadn't had convincing arguments.
   4) Wenn es schneien würde, könnten wir einen Schneemann bauen.
      If it was snowing, we could build a snowman.
   5) Wenn sie nicht sofort aufhören, solchen Lärm zu machen, hole ich die Polizei.
      If they don't stop making such a noise immediately, I'll call the police.
   6) Sie können den Pokal vergessen, wenn sie dieses Spiel nicht gewinnen.
      They can forget about the cup if they don't win this match.

5. **"Our languages are the reflections of ourselves." (ll. 7f.) Discuss this idea in class. Use the results of your discussion to write an essay on the subject.**

Our languages are the reflections of ourselves

Our language is a means of expressing our own perception of ourselves and the world around us. Things only become real and have a clear structure or definition if we can name and describe them. Therefore two people will never give exactly the same description of one object or of one event because they will concentrate on different details or think different things important. The colour turquoise, for example, will be described as "greenish-blue" by some and as "bluish-green" by others depending on the individual's perception.

The same is true for more abstract things like our emotions. Different people will express their emotions differently.

The way someone describes things also depends on their character, their family background and their education. A more educated person has a wider range of words and expressions at their command and is therefore able to be more precise.

The social and geographical surroundings in which we grow up also affect the way we express ourselves. Someone having grown up in a town will see and express things differently from someone having grown up in a secluded village.

So character, education and social and geographical background all influence one's language. The language someone uses gives in turn a lot of information about who they are and where they are from.

These mechanisms are not in operation at the same level while speaking a foreign language, so we can never be as precise and detailed as in our own language, which puts us in a disadvantage compared to native speakers.

6. **Imagine you had been among the audience at Benaras University. What would you like to tell Gandhi about the issue of anarchy? Write a letter explaining your opinion.**

Dear Mr Gandhi,

I was present at Benaras University when you made the moving speech about how our language is a means of expressing and forming a person's personality at the same time, and how vital it is for the building of a nation to speak one's native language.

You also talked about the issue of anarchy in our country and I totally agree with what you said.

I am myself an ardent nationalist and I want India to be free from her oppressors at last but we must not give in to the illusion that violence will bring about Indian independence more quickly. Certainly the use of violence would attract and appeal to all those who are deeply dissatisfied with the situation in present-day India and who have been wronged by our British oppressors. The use of violence would probably help to win several battles and perhaps even the war against the British but it would not help to build a free and united India after the British have left. On the contrary, it would leave us with destruction and division beyond repair, for the bomb that attacks the British oppressor will also kill the innocent Indian, whose family will never be able to forgive his murderers, even though they are their fellow-countrymen.

Violence can never be the foundation of a free and democratic country and therefore we must never use it in our noble fight!

We must carry on in our non-violent resistance against the British and even if it takes us twice as long to reach our aim, we will finally reach it. And then we will be able to look back with pride and satisfaction on the days of hardship and struggle.

Yours
XXXXXXXXX
a great admirer and supporter of your fight

My Two Lives

Jhumpa Lahiri

Author and text

Jhumpa Lahiri was born in London in 1967 to Indian parents. She was brought up in South Kingstown, Rhode Island, America. As her mother wanted to raise her children to be Indian, Jhumpa learned about her Bengali heritage from an early age. She graduated from South Kingstown High School and later received her BA in English Literature from Barnard College in 1989. She then received multiple degrees from Boston University: an MA in English, an MA in Creative Writing, an MA in Comparative Literature and a PhD in Renaissance Studies.

In 2000 she was awarded the Pulitzer Prize for Fiction.

Lahiri currently lives in Brooklyn with her husband and two children. She has been a Vice President of the PEN American Center since 2005. Her stories deal with the lives of Indians in exile, of people being torn between traditional Indians customs and those of the of Western world.

In this article Jhumpa Lahiri reflects on what it means to be brought up and to live in two cultures. She talks about experiences as a child of Indian parents being brought up in the US and switching between the Indian and American culture. She also thinks about the role her parents play in her life as an "Indian-American".

Solutions

Activities p. 50

1. Write a short biographical sketch for Jhumpa Lahiri based on the information given in the text. Then add more information about the writer. The following Internet address might be of help:

www.postcolonialweb.org/india/literature/lahiri/bio.html

Jhumpa Lahiri spent the first two years of her life in London, and then moved to the US, where she has been living ever since. She grew up in Rhode Island in the 1970s. Unlike most of her friends she didn't attend Sunday school, but instead, from time to time disappeared to India for months at a time. Her first book was published in 1999. She married her husband in Calcutta and has children.

Additional information: see "Author and text".

2. Examine her life as an Indian girl in America.

As Jhumpa has an Indian cultural background, her life in America is special. Though the term "Indian-American" is used to describe her, in her youth she felt neither Indian nor American (l. 7). She rather felt torn between what she perceived as the two sides of the hyphen; she felt the necessity to be loyal to both worlds, India (being the old world) and America (being the new world). She also felt torn between her parents and their way of life – speaking Bengali, eating rice and dal with one's fingers – and the American way of life she was confronted with, school, music, books, television and speaking English. Although she lived and spoke like her American friends, it was always obvious that she was not entirely American (l. 25). Many of the things absolutely natural to American children like attending Sunday school and ice-skating were unfamiliar to her. Apart from having a different name and different looks, she often disappeared to India for months at a time (l. 27).

3. Describe her parents' role in her development.

Jhumpa's parents have had a very strong influence on her development. They familiarized her with Indian culture and tradition, attaching great importance to their daughter acquiring and keeping the awareness and sense of being Indian. "I am Indian thanks to the efforts of two individuals. I feel Indian not because of the time I've spent in India or because of my genetic composition but rather because of my parents' steadfast presence in my life" (ll. 59–62). Her parents are responsible for the fact that Jhumpa doesn't lose track of being Indian. As long as they are alive they make sure that both parts in her, the American and the Indian, stay in balance. But she already knows that the American part in her will be dominant when her parents are not with her any longer.

4. **Trace her attitude towards being an "Indian-American" in the course of her life. To what extent does her attitude towards the hyphen change?**

   When Jhumpa was a small girl, she felt neither Indian nor American (l. 4) even if the term "Indian-American" was used to describe her. In contrast to some of her friends who were proud of being "Irish-American" or "Italian-American" (l. 28) she didn't feel positive about it. Whereas the other children seemed to be able to combine two different cultures, she always had the feeling of having nothing at all in the end, of being reduced to zero by the force of the two cultures shaping her. When Lahiri grew older and began to write, the term "Indian-American" developed a new meaning for her. In fact this term has become part of America's vocabulary (l. 41), everybody uses it and it seems clear to everybody what it means. Even Lahiri herself uses it now to describe her background without feeling the need to explain its notion any further, which makes her happy.

   As an adult, the feeling she had as a girl of being left destitute by the two cultures defining her has completely vanished. Now Jhumpa Lahiri has the rewarding feeling of gaining positive aspects from both cultures. She perceives the Indian and the American culture as being equal forces coexisting in a balanced and harmonious way, enriching her life.

5. **Explain the importance of writing for Jhumpa Lahiri.**

   Writing is of essential importance for Jhumpa Lahiri. She took to writing at a time when she was at grips with her cultural make-up. As she wasn't able, when younger, to tackle the situation of being influenced by two cultures, she tried to solve the problem by writing. Literature was a means of achieving in fiction what was denied to her in real life. What helped Lahiri in the past will also help her in the future; already now she is sure that writing will help her to interpret the notion of being Indian-American when her parents won't serve as a counterbalance to the American part any more. Fiction, Lahiri is convinced, will help her deal with the imbalance created by the loss of her parents and the Indianness they embody.

6. **Reflect on Lahiri's statement that "a bicultural upbringing is a rich but imperfect thing".**

   Growing up in two cultures can have advantages as well as disadvantages. One advantage certainly lies in the fact that the individual is shaped by two cultures at the same time. Traditions, customs, and ways of life from two sides are transmitted to the individual. But sometimes the individual doesn't want to show people this double influence and would rather hide the effect caused by a bicultural upbringing.

   In Lahiri's case the bicultural upbringing caused her pain when she was a girl. She tried very hard to be perfect in both cultures, but always had the feeling of not being a member in either. This led to the consequence that she denied herself an identity. Only as an adult can she admit to herself that the bicultural upbringing is imperfect. She takes elements from both cultures and gathers them in her personality. Yet there are aspects that she doesn't embody. As an adult she is able to analyze and to accept this. Lahiri herself gives the example of her proficiency in Bengali: her Indian background enables her to speak Bengali with her own children, but her knowledge of the language isn't adequate for her to be able to teach her children to read and write Bengali. She has an imperfect proficiency of Bengali.

7. **Familiarize yourself with Lahiri's novel *The Namesake*. To what extent are Lahiri's personal experiences reflected in the novel? Pay special attention to gender questions as the protagonist in *The Namesake* is a man.**

Summary:

The novel begins with the birth of Gogol, the main character. The reader is given background information on the lives of both Gogol's parents (Ashima and Ashoke Ganguli) and each character's story is told from his or her own perspective. Ashima and Ashoke grew up in Calcutta, India. They came to America as young adults right after they were married. Ashima, in particular, had a difficult time adjusting to American society. From the very beginning the issue of names and identity is presented. It is explained that members of this culture are given two names: one that is a pet name (used only by family and close friends) and one that is used by the rest of society. At birth, Gogol is given a pet name as his official name because his official name from his grandmother was lost in the post. As a child, Gogol is told by his family that he is to be called Nikhil by teachers and the other children at school. Gogol rejects his proper name and wants to be called Gogol by his family *and* society. This one decision, on the first day of kindergarten causes him years of distress, though it is also his first attempt to reject a dual identity. This importance of names and identity is brought up throughout the story and is a concept that is central to the novel.

Throughout his life Gogol suffers greatly from the uniqueness of his name. In Bengali families, "individual names are sacred, inviolable. They are not meant to be inherited or shared". However, Gogol spends his life living in the United States where children are often ashamed of their differences from others. In adolescence, Gogol wants to blend in and live unnoticed. This presents a struggle between two cultures. The Ganguli's wish is to raise Gogol and his younger sister with Bengali cultural values. On the other hand Gogol and Sonia grow up relating mostly to their peers and the surrounding culture in the United States.

Gogol is ashamed of his name throughout high school. Being away from home at college makes it easy for Gogol to live as Nikhil in the American culture, detaching himself from his roots and his family as much as possible.

Gogol graduates college planning to live life as Nikhil. He enters a relationship (with Maxine) where he throws himself into an American family who has little worry or concern about life. He lives in their care-free atmosphere. This lasts until Nikhil gets a stab in the heart that sends him home, finally, as Gogol, causing Nikhil to begin to mesh with Gogol to form one identity. Gogol is drawn back to the one place he has avoided for so many years. Even Maxine can no longer change his mind.

Gogol's final relationship in the novel is one not only accepted by his family, but indeed positively encouraged. Moushumi was the daughter of Ganguli's good friends. He marries Moushumi as Gogol and accepts his family and his culture completely again. He learns that the answer is not to abandon or attempt to diminish either culture, but to mesh the two together. Gogol is not fully in tune with his identity until he realizes that it is embellished by both cultures. He does not have to be one or the other, he is made up of both and instead of weakening, his pride is strengthened. Though the novel wraps up with other misfortunes occurring in Gogol's life, he is able to stand up on his own two feet. He is proud of who he is and where he comes from. Most importantly, he is proud of his name and all that it means. Lahiri provides detailed descriptions of heartache, grief, love and joy, which are all part of every human's identity.

As we can see from the summary, Lahiri's personal problems of divided identity, belonging and bicultural upbringing are reflected in the novel. The fact that the novel's protagonist is a man is of no importance. The questions that are raised about immigration and its consequences are not gender-specific but universally human.

Klausur

(Un)arranged Marriage

Bali Rai

In this excerpt, the protagonist (Manjit) and his father are watching a live football match on TV.

[...] The game was open [...], but I could feel my dad and his blood-shot eyes glaring[1] as I tried to keep my mind on the game.

"Manjit, I am talking to you". His voice was supercalm, which was a pleasant surprise.

5 "Yes, Daddy-ji, I replied [...].

"I have spoken to a friend of mine in India, about his daughter". He paused for a moment. I think maybe he was waiting for me to say something. To react. But I just kept my eyes on the game and wondered what he was going to say next, about what he had agreed with his friend in India. I knew that it had to be about marriage because it had

10 been exactly the same when he had told (my brother) Harry. We had been in the back garden playing Badminton [...]. Harry had been getting all upset because I'd been making him look like the big whale that he was. He'd been all sweaty and out of breath when my dad walked up and told Harry that he was going to get married to the girl whose photo he had seen the week before. Just like that. My dad had already sorted

15 everything out. They'd shown Harry a photo of the girl, dressed up in traditional gear[2] and wearing too much make-up, then told him that it was *his* choice. They wanted *him* to make a decision – yes or no. It was all a con[3] really. Harry didn't really have a choice, or the opportunity to say no. All the decisions were made for him by my dad and the girl's father. Harry had known what his answer *had* to be. And, for Harry, it was prob-

20 ably the only way he'd ever *get* a girl, anyway.

Thing is, I was totally different to Harry. Totally. And there was no way that I was going to say "yes" to marrying some girl from India just by looking at a photo of her. No way. So I began to concentrate really hard on the football, even though my mind was all over the place, and much of what my old man said at first went in one ear, and straight

25 out the other. I was hearing but not listening. I managed about five minutes before the old man's words started to cause my stomach to turn over. He was talking about *me*. And some *girl. From India*. He already had it all sorted out just like it had been with Harry. All that remained was the wedding itself. She was six month older than me and coming over to England on a visitor's visa in July. Two months away!

30 "I have told her father that you will marry her after next summer, when you are both seventeen. If we leave it any longer there will be too many questions from the immigration people. Once you are married she will have the right to stay in this country and I will have my final daughter-in-law.

The look on my face must have said everything that I was thinking. My palms were

35 getting all sweaty and I wanted to get out of the house. Just run. Be anywhere but where I was at the moment. I wanted to scream at him and shout and swear. Hit him. But I couldn't do anything. My legs felt like they were frozen [...]. My mind was all

---

[1]**to glare** to look angrily at   [2]**gear** a set of clothes you wear for a particular occasion or activity   [3]**con** Schwindel

jumbled up [...]. I was in trouble. My dad obviously saw my reaction because he changed his lecture to one about how it was my duty to uphold his honour, his *izzat*. To protect the family and all that.   40

"I don't want to be like the other men that they laugh at [...]: the ones whose sons and daughters have run away and become druggies and prostitutes, or married unsuitable people – Muslims and Hindus and *goreh* or, God forbid, *kaleh*[4]. That is not why your mother and me brought you on to this earth. To ruin our name and rubbish our *izzat*. We brought you up to be a good Punjabi. And I won't let you ruin it all because you 45 think that you are something different from us. Something special. Blood will always be blood, Manjit. And your colour will always be your colour. Look in the mirror. You are a Punjabi, not a *gorah*. You are not from this country, even if you were born here. These people are not the same as us. They are not the same. We have to protect our culture, Manjit. Our way of life. And do not think that I am stupid, Manjit. I have seen 50 the way that you have been headed[5] recently. Stealing and messing about at school. I found a cigarette in your room last week. You think that I will let you carry on this way? Ruining my name. No!"

I could see his anger beginning to rise up in him, like he was about to explode. His face was going red all over and the little blood vessels that he had on his cheeks and 55 over his nose [...] were showing more clearly than normal. My mum had come into the room and she sat down opposite me. I could tell from her face that she was about to launch into the kind of hysterics that she had gone with Harry, emotional blackmail[6] before he said "yes". And he had *wanted* to have an arranged marriage. Just to get a girl.   60

"Your poor mother has cooked and cleaned for you all these years. Wiped your backside and fed you. Think of her when you are out with that *kalah* of yours, smoking and chasing dirty white girls. Think of her and what the neighbours say to her when they see you walking around on Evington Road like a tramp. A criminal. Smoking your cigarettes in front of our relatives and friends, with no shame. What do you think you 65 are, Manjit? Why do you think that I will let you be the one to ruin our name, when all of your brothers and sisters have not? [...] Do you want to kill me? Is it that? Do you want to kill your mother?"

Almost on the cue, my mum started crying and calling out to God. It was all "Hai Rabbah" (Oh God) and slapping her thighs the way that Punjabi women do at funerals. I 70 already knew that she was gonna do that – knew that she was just putting on an act to scare me into accepting their way of doing things. But even knowing this, seeing my mum crying and wailing made me feel guilty and upset, just like I was supposed to. [...] In the end I ended up crying too because I didn't know what I was going to do. I felt like I was stuck. Like I had no choice.   75

From: Bali Rai, *(Un)arranged Marriage*, published by Corgi, London 2001, reprinted by permission of The Random House Group Ltd.

---

[4]**gorah** *(singular)*, **goreh** *(plural)* a white person, white people; **kalah** *(singular)* **kaleh** *(plural)*: a black person, black people   [5]**to be headed** to go in an certain direction   [6]**emotional blackmail** to make s. o. feel guilty

Klausur

Activities

1. Work out who Majit is.

2. Describe what state of mind Majit is in after his father has told him about his plan. Trace the different steps in Majit's feelings.

3. Characterize Majit's parents and work out the role they play in his life.

4. Creative writing:
   Majit's brother, Harry, has had an arranged marriage too. Unlike Majit, Harry was not really against an arranged marriage. He puts forward arguments in favour of having an arranged marriage in order to comfort his younger brother, who, however, can't be comforted. Work out a dialogue between the two brothers taking into consideration the information given about them in the text.

Klausur Solution

1. Work out who Majit is.

Majit is a 16-year-old Punjabi teenager living in Britain with his family. He seems to be interested in sports, especially football. As we learn from his father's reproaches, Majit has recently had a lot of problems: there is trouble at school, Majit seems to have stolen something and he is secretly smoking as can be seen by the cigarette found in his room.

Furthermore he seems to have a black friend with whom he goes out and meets girls – white girls. All this makes his father very angry. Majit is going to have an arranged marriage with a girl from India whom he hasn't seen before. His own father and the girl's father have already arranged everything.

Majit has an older brother. Harry is already married to an Indian girl through an arranged marriage, some time ago. But unlike for Majit himself, the arranged marriage was for Harry, according to Majit, the only way to get married, as Harry doesn't seem to be particularly attractive.

2. Describe what state of mind Majit is in after his father has told him about his plan. Trace the different steps in Majit's feelings.

Majit is watching TV when his father confronts him with the marriage plans. In a first phase Majit tries to ignore the news, staring intensely at the TV. The events that happened in a comparable situation, when his brother Harry was informed about an arranged marriage some time ago, go through his mind. He relives this situation without noticing at first that, in this instance, *he* is the person concerned. Only after some minutes does he realize that his future life is being decided upon by his father this very moment.

When he finally gets the point in a second phase, he is shocked and shows strong physical reactions: his stomach turns over and he begins to sweat. Apart from these physical reactions he wants to flee to be far away from where he actually is. He also feels like screaming, shouting, swearing and hitting his father. But as a matter of fact he isn't able to do anything. It is as if he is paralyzed.

In a third phase, when his father changes his strategy, now causing Majit to have a guilty conscience and insulting him, Majit feels guilty and upset. When his mother enters the room and starts to cry, showing that she is suffering because of her son's behaviour, Majit starts to cry too.

3. Characterize Majit's parents and work out the role they play in his life.

Majit's parents are two completely different persons. Whereas his father is loud and boastful, his mother is less talkative.

Majit's father is a Punjabi who seems to care a great deal about Indian traditions. He attaches great importance to the fact that his family, especially his children, apply them although they live in Britain where they were born. Indian values such as upholding one's honour and protecting the family range among the most important things in his life. There are clear dos and don'ts for him and his family to stick to. The usage of Indian words for key concepts, such as *izzat*, honour, show this tendency very clearly. But at the same time, he is rather egocentric. Though he talks a lot about protecting the family, he doesn't care in the least about his sons' well-being but rather about his own. What neighbours and relatives think and say is more important to him than how his children feel. Obviously Majit is well-integrated and has

Klausur Solution

non-Punjabi friends – a fact that his father doesn't tolerate at all. He acts like an absolute monarch whom one has to obey. Majit's mother is only able to enforce her husband's argumentation without saying a single word herself. Her husband does the talking for her and only uses her to intensify his argumentation.

Although father and mother are so different, they are a perfect match when it comes to influencing and intimidating their son Majit. He seems to be completely dependent on them.

4. Creative writing:
Majit's brother, Harry, has had an arranged marriage. Unlike Majit, Harry was not really against an arranged marriage. He puts forward arguments in favour of having an arranged marriage in order to comfort his younger brother, who, however, can't be comforted. Work out a dialogue between the two brothers taking into consideration the information given about them in the text.

The dialogue could be based on the following arguments:

arguments put forward by Harry	arguments put forward by Majit
– Comfortable way to get a wife – Parents know their children; they only want their best. – Parents have enough experience to provide the best for their children. – After some time one gets used to the chosen girl. – You don't have to worry about anything: no dating problems, no need to organize the wedding. – You can just rely on others. – In most cases you don't risk getting rejected by the girl. – You are sure to get sb decent.	– He is too young. – Need to be independent – Need to get out and have fun – He does not want to feel as if he is in prison. – He wants to find a girl on his own. – Arranged marriage might be ok for someone unattractive (Harry!!!), but unthinkable for others. – He wants to live his own life, not the one decided upon by parents. – Britain and Western values count more than Indian values which are strange to him. – He feels like an English person since he was born and raised in Britain. – India and Indian traditions are unknown to him.

Discover ...

Shakespeare-Textausgaben
Landeskundliche Themenhefte

Herausgegeben von
Klaus Hinz und Engelbert Thaler (ab 2007)

Africa – Postcolonial Experiences
Von Monika Teichmann
70 S.   Best.-Nr. **978-3-14-040100-5**
Lehrerheft.   Best.-Nr. **978-3-14-040101-2**

African-American Experiences – From Exploitation to Participation
Von Wiltrud Frenken, Angela Luz und Brigitte Prischtt
55 S.   Best.-Nr. **978-3-14-040116-6**
Lehrerheft.   Best.-Nr. **978-3-14-040117-3**

Australia and New Zealand – Neither Down nor Under
Von Rainer H. Berthelmann
95 S.   Best.-Nr. **978-3-14-040104-3**
Lehrerheft.   Best.-Nr. **978-3-14-040105-0**

British and American Youth Culture
Von Hannspeter Bauer und Gudrun Vesper
64 S.   Best.-Nr. **978-3-14-040053-4**
Lehrerheft.   Best.-Nr. **978-3-14-040077-0**

Canada – More than Mounties and Lumberjacks
Von Martin Kohn
56 S.   Best.-Nr. **978-3-14-040082-4**
Lehrerheft.   Best.-Nr. **978-3-14-040092-3**

Globalisation – Blessing or Curse?
Von Jürgen Einhoff, Klaus Hinz und Karl Heinz Wagner
68 S.   Best.-Nr. **978-3-14-040059-6**
Lehrerheft.   Best.-Nr. **978-3-14-040089-3**

Hispanics in America
Von Veronika Kaiser und James Martin
72 S.   Best.-Nr. **978-3-14-040044-2**
Lehrerheft.   Best.-Nr. **978-3-14-040064-0**

India – Tradition and Transformation
Von Michaela Banzhaf und Alexandra Peschel
51 S.   Best.-Nr. **978-3-14-040098-5**
Lehrerheft.   Best.-Nr. **978-3-14-040099-2**

Ireland – Changes and Challenges
Von Maria Eisenmann
55 S.   Best.-Nr. **978-3-14-040110-4**
Lehrerheft.   Best.-Nr. **978-3-14-040111-1**

Our Environment – A State of Emergency?
Von Stephen Speight
59 S.   Best.-Nr. **978-3-14-040108-1**
Lehrerheft.   Best.-Nr. **978-3-14-040109-8**

The American Dream – Inventing a Nation
Von Hanspeter Bauer
74 S.   Best.-Nr. **978-3-14-040086-2**
Lehrerheft.   Best.-Nr. **978-3-14-040087-9**

The American South
Von Jürgen Einhoff und Katharina Einhoff
72 S.   Best.-Nr. **978-3-14-040052-7**
Lehrerheft.   Best.-Nr. **978-3-14-040076-3**

The Different Faces of Britain
Von Stephen Speight
64 S.   Best.-Nr. **978-3-14-040085-5**
Lehrerheft.   Best.-Nr. **978-3-14-040095-4**

The Fascination and Risks of Technology
Von Stephen Speight
56 S.   Best.-Nr. **978-3-14-040055-8**
Lehrerheft.   Best.-Nr. **978-3-14-040079-4**

The Mass Media – From Gutenberg to Gates
Von Stephen Speight und Karsten Witsch
64 S.   Best.-Nr. **978-3-14-040088-6**
Lehrerheft.   Best.-Nr. **978-3-14-040096-1**

William Shakespeare: A Midsummer Night's Dream
Von Rainer Gocke und Angela Stock
104 S.   Best.-Nr. **978-3-14-040058-9**
Lehrerheft.   Best.-Nr. **978-3-14-040068-8**

William Shakespeare: Macbeth
Von Rainer Gocke und Angela Stock
136 S.   Best.-Nr. **978-3-14-040041-1**
Lehrerheft.   Best.-Nr. **978-3-14-040061-9**

William Shakespeare: Much Ado About Nothing
Von Rainer Gocke und Franziska Quabeck
110 S.   Best.-Nr. **978-3-14-040118-0**
Lehrerheft.   Best.-Nr. **978-3-14-040119-7**

William Shakespeare: Othello
Von Anke Weber
147 S.   Best.-Nr. **978-3-14-040069-5**
Lehrerheft.   Best.-Nr. **978-3-14-040102-9**

William Shakespeare: Romeo and Juliet
Von Norbert Timm
143 S.   Best.-Nr. **978-3-14-040056-5**
Lehrerheft.   Best.-Nr. **978-3-14-040081-7**

William Shakespeare: The Sonnets
Von Anke Weber
48 S.   Best.-Nr. **978-3-14-040114-2**
Lehrerheft.   Best.-Nr. **978-3-14-040115-9**

William Shakespeare: Bits From The Bard
Nach Themenschwerpunkten zusammengestellt
Von Norbert Timm
48 S.   Best.-Nr. **978-3-14-040057-2**
Lehrerheft.   Best.-Nr. **978-3-14-040097-8**

Weitere Titel sind in Vorbereitung.

Schöningh Verlag
Postfach 2540
33055 Paderborn

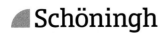

Fordern Sie unseren Prospekt zur kompletten Reihe an:
Informationen 0800 / 18 18 787 (freecall)
info@schoeningh-schulbuch.de / www.schoeningh-schulbuch.de